SEEING YOURSELF
IN THE
M I R R O R
OF
M A R R I A G E

JAMES DUBBS

WESTBOW
PRESS®
A DIVISION OF THOMAS NELSON
& ZONDERVAN

WestBow Press books may be ordered through booksellers or by contacting:

WestBow Press
A Division of Thomas Nelson & Zondervan
1663 Liberty Drive
Bloomington, IN 47403
www.westbowpress.com
844-714-3454

ISBN: 978-1-6642-9312-0 (sc)
ISBN: 978-1-6642-9313-7 (hc)
ISBN: 978-1-6642-9311-3 (e)

Library of Congress Control Number: 2023903200

Print information available on the last page.

WestBow Press rev. date: 04/04/2023

DEDICATION

To Joni, my wife of fifty-four years and counting. I could not have a better partner, for it wasn't long into marriage before we discovered ourselves so different in many ways yet so alike in other ways, which revealed problems—both ways. But through mutual commitment, we partnered to work on ourselves. That cooperative and collective effort rescued our marriage.

To this point, we have been blessed with five beautiful daughters (Jodi, Jamie, Joy, Julie, and Jill), three respectful and responsible sons-in-law (Kyle Anderson, Todd Broschart, and Sterling Montague III), and thirteen action-packed grandchildren (Ethan, Sean, Molly, Emily, Luke, Lacey, Brittain, April, Jolie, Sterling IV, Duke, Wendy, and Flynn). Sweetheart, our quiver is full (Psalm 127:5). All of you have enriched my life beyond anything I could have imagined, and it is with delight and love that I dedicate this work in honor of my family and all its offshoots.

CONTENTS

PREFACE

I have maintained an ongoing counseling ministry for more than five decades of public ministry as a youth pastor and a senior pastor. From my perspective, I see a pastor's counseling ministry as being somewhat different and unique from the efforts of other counselors, whether in a secular or non-clergy religious setting.

As a pastor, one becomes a shepherd of God's sheep (His people), whom God has entrusted to a pastor's watchful care. More accurately, the pastor is the under-shepherd, and Christ is the chief Shepherd. As a Pastor I would find myself intertwined in various lives of those I shepherded, and particularly, the ones I counseled. This Pastoral arrangement can differ from other counselors, who may see clients in the confines of an office setting for an hour or so each week and any number of counseling sessions as needed or desired.

I have found that a pastor-shepherd's vantage point can result in more overall exposure to the ones being counseled. This view often provides a pastor with a holistic perspective to the true nature of a counselee's problem(s). In this setting, counselees may relate information and viewpoints about the problems they firmly believe to be true. Yet their assessment may be inaccurate in light of what the pastoral counselor has observed from the larger picture, which is gained by viewing counselees in various settings. Quite often, those life settings reveal a number of personality traits, shortcomings, and salient issues in the life and relationships of the counselee during interaction with others.

Granted, such detail was not available to me in many of those I counseled. But I have benefited enough times from such opportunities that I have become keenly aware of how hard it is for many of us to see ourselves as we really are, to face ourselves, and to own our shortcomings, which quite often will surface as problem areas in our relationships. Over time, for various ones I counseled, I witnessed family dynamics at work and observed marriages up close and personal, as a dinner guest in their homes, while sharing church work projects, or being a part of the same social gatherings. In addition, I saw how counselees interacted with friends and fellow parishioners. All these observations enhanced my insights and influenced my counseling directives and conclusions. These practical experiences added to and honed my skill set, which had been acquired through formal training. I was not formally trained as a psychologist or psychiatrist but as a pastor with a Bible college and seminary background, equipped with a working knowledge of the Scriptures that lay out God's interaction with His Creation, and His dealings with fallen man. No one knows us better than our Creator, and nothing can better "solve" us and our problems than His conclusions and directives.

As I became more heavily involved in a counseling ministry, I committed to strengthening my counseling skills through numerous training opportunities, both secular and religious. I never financially charged for my counseling services, for I saw it as a part of my ministry. Perhaps providing counseling at no charge was one reason I was kept busy. But in that busyness and though difficult at times, I have thoroughly enjoyed the opportunities in trying to help others attain marital success.

From a pastoral vantage point and my own years of marriage, I write this book. I present thoughts from where the rubber meets the road while considering *Bible truth intersecting with marital reality.* At this crossroad of seeing and facing themselves, spouses can find significant help, both as individual participants in marriage and as couples united in marriage.

ACKNOWLEDGMENTS

I thank my Lord, who did a work in my wife and me, which caused us to strive for and thrive in our marriage relationship.

I thank my daughters, Jodi and Joy, who, for hours, sat with me and brought focus to the work. They recognized and suggested material I needed to include, exclude, and pare down from the reams of writings I had penned on marriage.

I thank Marilyn Harris, who willingly put in the time and effort to read this manuscript and add her expertise in editing and organization.

I thank Patricia Wood, and Pam Lagamarsino, who brought years of editing experience, expertise, and encouragement to this project.

INTRODUCTION

"My wife and I have been married for over a hundred years" is a line I have often used when introducing my three-point marriage homily to a bride and groom while conducting a wedding ceremony. The audience chuckles, and I then explain that marriage has been fifty-plus years for me and fifty-plus years for my wife. Although you might chuckle as well, there may be a kernel of truth in my opening line. After all, there are two perspectives, and those two different vantage points merge together as an ongoing part of the marriage experience. The myriad of up-and-down feelings and experiences that are part of marriage could leave us feeling like one's marriage has been a long haul.

It is hopeful that the many shared experiences result mostly in an accumulation of happy and beneficial reflections for both people, even in the difficult experiences of life and marriage, which a couple encounters together. If a couple learns to positively embrace things together, they can experience a togetherness that *each* can cherish. In doing so, they will discover marriage as it ought to be—as God intended it to be.

CHAPTER 1

The Cause of Marital Discord

USUALLY, SEVERAL TRAITS OR FEATURES one individual sees in another can spark feelings and preferences, lead to romance, and result in marriage. When one is smitten, it doesn't take long for those several traits or features to balloon into a long list of self-convincing reinforcement, which cries out, *This could be the one!* Many people consider physical attraction between two individuals as the initial attention-getter. Yet others are first drawn to another person's personality, a caring spirit, or a carefree and fun-loving persona. Some are attracted to that shy introvert, and others are attracted to the interactive extrovert. One would think that if a person married the one to whom they were attracted, whatever the attraction was, wedded bliss would be the outcome. Unfortunately, it often isn't the result. Why?

During my college years in the mid 60's, the husband-wife duet of Sonny and Cher performed the pop song, "I Got You, Babe." In 1965 this hit climbed to number one on the pop charts. It idolized the love they had for each other. I remember their fans saw them as the darlings of our day. They were young, charismatic, energetic, and talented. The duo was featured on talk shows and magazine covers. Together, they projected the face of young, committed love. After nine years of marriage, their divorce was finalized in 1975. What happened?

Also in the same year that Sonny and Cher's marriage ended, another married couple came to the musical forefront. Captain and Tennille captured the pop nation's attention by singing the love song that climbed to number one on the pop charts that year, "Love Will Keep Us Together." Yet after thirty-nine years of marriage, they divorced in 2014. Why?

A Key Component of Marital Failure or Success

Why have there been so many divorces throughout culture, be they singers, Hollywood starlets, politicians, businesspeople, parents, white-collar workers, blue-collar workers, the young, the middle-aged, the old, the rich, the poor, the middle-class, the secular, or the religious? Many are divorcing for the first time. Others are divorcing for the second or even third time or beyond that. Two past Hollywood starlets have each married eight different times, and one currently has married nine times! It doesn't matter what your background, religion, color, ethnicity, or status in life is; your chances for marriage ending in divorce are high. Divorce in today's America has become an avalanche!

People usually marry because they think they are in love. I assume that most newly married couples expect to live together happily for the rest of their days. Why doesn't love keep many of them together? After all, Sonny and Cher sang, "I Got You, Babe." Well, that becomes a key component of the problem. I got *you*, babe—all of you, warts included—and you have me, babe—all of me. If love fails to keep so many couples together, what separates them?

A love-smitten individual may initially identify a number of good qualities in his or her potential spouse, which leads to marriage. Throughout the marriage, that list may gradually be replaced with another list, which is just as long, if not longer. And what is the new list about? *All the reasons I am done with you, babe!* An accumulation of irritations, nasty habits, inconsiderate actions, and other offensive activity surface in one spouse, which negatively impacts the other spouse and may prove too much for the impacted and offended spouse to overcome, or be even willing to try.

What happens? Over time, the unwelcomed actions being exposed or becoming more pronounced in the offending spouse can turn toxic in the marriage. If either spouse is unwilling to address his or her own offensive problems and reduce them—or better yet, work at eliminating them—marital bliss will prove hard to achieve. What about couples who *do* stay together and in love throughout a lifetime? Is the conscientious overhauling of one's wrongful ways, undertaken by each spouse, their secret to success?

Herein is what I have found. "Marriage doesn't *create* problems; it *reveals* problems" is a declaration that revolutionized my marriage after I heard it many years ago in the early stage of my marriage. I cannot say with certainty where I heard it, but I believe it was from a cassette tape presentation I heard in the early 1970's by the late Dr. Howard Hendricks, a professor at Dallas Theological Seminary. Although I could not document the source of the statement, I have come to recognize and appreciate the wisdom within the sentence. If the source was Dr. Hendricks, I want to give credit where credit is due. Some suggest Pastor Rick Warren is the author of the quote I heard, but since he is eight years younger than I, he would have been a teenager when I heard the quote early into my marriage.

In fleshing out this nugget when conducting marriage counseling, I explain it in the following manner. The problems of their marriage will be the problems each partner brings to the union. If each person works on himself or herself and does not shift to focus on the partner's shortcomings, there is a high probability of marital success.

Some would argue the opposite is true. They believe marriage *is* the problem and source of a maelstrom of difficulties undeservedly visited on them, which are brought into an individual's life by a spouse or an ex. They blame the shortcomings and misconduct of a spouse for virtually all marital woes. They often have a never-my-fault view or a mostly-not-my-fault perspective.

If such a mindset describes you, this book will challenge you to examine your marriage conclusions when confronted with facts about you and the things most all intuitively know about the human experience. Read on and accept the invitation (and challenge) to see yourself and your marriage in a new light and from a different perspective, as you look into the marriage mirror. You will find that the Bible and life's experiences converge to reveal the needed truth about each partner in a marital relationship.

Allow me to clarify here. Although I believe marriage doesn't create problems but reveals them in each partner, there are situations where problems can surface because of the marriage experience. For example, before being married, I had no problem with my choice of mattress. I like a firm mattress, whereas my wife enjoys a soft mattress. While I was single, mattress choice was a nonissue because I could choose the mattress that suited me. I entered marriage, and now my wife and I must figure out how to solve a mattress dilemma. In this sense, marriage can create problems that individuals would otherwise not have to face if they were single. But such problems need not rise to the level of destroying a marriage—unless allowed to do so.

Solve Yourself, Not Your Mate

At the destructive level, unresolved problems within each spouse too often become the culprits in a failing marriage. A stubborn or selfish refusal by my wife or me to work together by working on our individual selves to resolve the mattress issue or any other issue would be the real culprit threatening the marriage. However, we must acknowledge that serious issues may arise in a marriage where a spouse personally exhibits such egregious behavior that even if he or she repents, such actions can destroy the marriage bond from the other spouse's perspective.

Engaging in extramarital affairs, living the life of a miscreant, or being a spousal abuser can sound the death knell to a marriage. Even allowing wrongful inaction to become chronic—such as a spouse no longer being affectionate or refusing to carry out everyday responsibilities—can erode the marital bond. Dysfunctional marriages can be destroyed by far lesser issues, due to personal problems not being worked through or left undone by both individuals in a marriage. Over time, such irresponsible inaction breeds criticism between spouses, and then charges and countercharges fly in the marriage.

In the book of Galatians, the apostle Paul warned against focusing on the wrongs of others. He said, "But if you bite and devour one another, take care that you are not consumed by one another" (Galatians 5:15). In the early years of our marriage, my wife and I fell prey to this destructive habit. Joni came into our marriage with a somewhat critical spirit—not of others but of me. I was puzzled (and annoyed) to see how well she accepted others for what and who they were, yet when it came to me, at times, I felt I could do little right in her eyes. I am not telling any tales out of school by alluding to her criticisms, for she readily admits to that past flaw. I admiringly say past flaw, for that is not her today, nor has it been her for a very long time.

I came into our marriage as an avoider. I was reared in an alcoholic's home, where conflict flared up when my father abused alcohol. To get out of the line of fire between my parents, I would either lie low or leave the house and hang out elsewhere. Again, I am not telling any tales out of school, for exposure of my father's battle with alcohol did not remain hidden behind the walls of our home.

In fairness to my father, he literally bore the scars of war on his back and legs. My mother shared with me that he was a tank commander in World War II, and he suffered major skin loss on both legs when his tank took an incoming mortar hit, which caused a flashfire inside the tank. Doctors took skin from his back and grafted it onto his legs. It's hard to imagine the gruesome agony he suffered from his physical wounds, the long, painful road to recovery, and the psychological damage that had been inflicted on him during the war.

In spite of living through the hard times when triggered by my father's abuse of alcohol, the other times created by my parents were of a loving and caring nature for their family – especially by my mother. I honor my deceased parents, and I salute my father's sacrifice for our country and the ancillary sacrifices my mother endured from marital discord, which was most likely exacerbated by the battlefields in Europe. But my parents' marital problems were not birthed in Europe but were developed within each of them, as is true within each of us.

A Recipe for Disaster

Let's fast-forward in time. My wife and I were now married, and it could easily have ended in disaster. Here was a woman who, at times, voiced her displeasure with me and about something I had done, which she didn't think I should have done or something I wasn't doing, which she thought I should be doing. In turn, she was dealing with a man who was an avoider—one who was perfecting the art of skipping his way through life while sidestepping and dodging unpleasantries. In our marriage, the more the newlywed wife criticized her husband, which at times, he rightly deserved, the more the newlywed husband avoided, walked away from, and stayed away from her, both physically and emotionally. These were not the only problems we brought to the marriage (more on that later).

Problem areas within a person's life can come from various sources. An individual's internal issues can develop from exposure to damaging family dynamics he or she was reared in, such as an alcoholic home or a home where parents played favorites among their children. Problems can form from a person's personality, such as an easygoing person allowing that laid-back persona to interfere with fulfilling responsibilities in a timely manner, which the delay may result in irritating others who are quick to do a task. Problems can form from within based on how one endures or handles trauma they suffered in life (as my father endeavored to offset by turning to alcohol, which made matters worse for him and his loved ones).

Regardless of the source of internal problem areas, the majority of solutions are found when each partner solves his or her own problems within. Couples won't find beneficial solutions and enjoy marriage as God intended when partners endeavor to relentlessly challenge and change each other's shortcomings. Even a habit of periodically confronting a spouse's shortcomings may wear thin in the partner who is challenged. What will you see in yourself when you look into the mirror of marriage and allow it to reflect you? Where is your focus? Does it remain on your spouse's shortcomings, or do you prioritize being all *you* should be as a beginning point of any marital hope? The more time you focus on your mate's inconsistencies and failures, the less time you'll have (or think you'll need) to spend on self-reflection and corrective effort.

Now, it is important to head off a possible misunderstanding. In my emphasis of having you look at yourself in your marriage, this book is not about throwing the reader under the bus by placing any and all blame on the reader for a myriad of marital woes. After all, *you're* the one reading the book and trying to find answers to better or salvage the marriage. The problems self-evaluation may reveal within and about you don't mean you bear sole responsibility for what might be a breaking or broken marriage. In actuality, you and your conduct may prove to play a minor role, if any, in a failing marriage. My appeal to you is about having you (and hopefully your spouse) engage in an honest assessment of personal conduct and character as part of the marital partnership, which will lead to a way of correcting what may be missing or amiss in any reader of this book.

A word of caution: Do not be quick to dismiss or excuse yourself as an equal partner in marital problems. To do so can be a disservice to your marriage, your mate, and yourself. If you have serious flaws that you cannot see or that you are unwilling to acknowledge, those will often travel with you into other relationships that you are part of. I have counseled enough individuals who were already part of second and third marriages that by the time they had come to me, their history of failed marriages left them willing to listen, which was unlike before when confronted or challenged by others who tried to help them. During times of struggle within their different marriages, the redundancy that prompted past marital failures has dawned on them—*they* might actually have been the "it" factor in those failures. Then many of these newly enlightened ones became willing to face themselves and deal with their far-too-long unaddressed shortcomings. Now there was hope for them.

How did Joni and I break the cycle of destructive behavior within ourselves? First, we had to have our eyes opened to our individual selves. Second, each of us had to humble ourselves by acknowledging the various shortcomings that each had brought. Third, we had to commit our minds and wills to do the necessary work for a successful, God-honoring marriage. The balance of this book speaks to that necessary work.

CHAPTER 2

A Fatal Flaw

WHILE CASUALLY SCANNING A TRAVEL blog, some fascinating details about the Great Wall of China caught my attention. To protect Chinese dynasties, China embarked on a Herculean effort, which encompassed two thousand years of construction. They built a wall along its northern borders to protect them against nomadic groups. The wall was 13,170.70 miles long.[1] The accomplishment was tabbed as one of the Seven Wonders of the World and one of the seven wonders of the medieval world. But the effort had a built-in, fatal flaw. As impregnable as the wall seemed to be against any enemy, it was breached, and defeat came to the land.

Genghis Khan (1162-1227), founder of the Mongolian empire, is reported to be the only one who breached the Great Wall of China in its 2,700-year history. In his lifetime, he led his Mongolian army to breach the Great Wall not only once but several times and at different locations along the wall. These successes were a big help in overthrowing the Jin Dynasty (1115-1234 AD) and the founding of the Yuan Dynasty (1271-1368

---

[1] Novakivska, Sonia. Fun Facts about Great Wall: 25 Things You Didn't Know," *Travel China Guide,* https://www.travelchinaguide.com/china_great_wall/facts/.

AD).[2] And how did the conqueror Khan breach the wall? He did so by bribing the gatekeepers within.

In applying these thoughts to marriage, couples must ever be aware of and stay diligent against potential dangers, both from outside and within one's marriage. Inattention to either or both may prove disastrous, but in light of the lesson to be learned from the bribed gatekeepers from within the wall of China, consider the findings of marriage specialist Dr. John Gottman. Dr. Gottman is director of the Gottman Institute. He is world-renowned for his work on marital stability and divorce prediction. Dr. Gottman has conducted forty years of breakthrough research with thousands of couples. He is the author of over two hundred published academic articles and of more than forty books.[3] He and his wife have been married for over thirty years. They are cofounders of the Gottman Institute.

In his writings, he speaks about what he calls "the four horsemen of divorce." This plays on the biblical reference of "the four horsemen of the apocalypse." Dr. Gottman's four horsemen of divorce are criticism, contempt, defensiveness, and stonewalling.[4] Of the four, he concludes that contempt is "the best predictor of divorce, and that while the other three horsemen occur in good marriages, and can be repaired, contempt is essentially zero in marriages that work well."[5] Based on my findings, I strongly concur that contempt will ravage a relationship more than any other negative action in a marriage. Contempt is a close cousin to

---

[2] "How did Genghis Khan Breach China's Great Wall?" *Travel China Guide*, https://www.travelchinaguide.com/china_great_wall/military-defense/genghis-khan.htm.

[3] "About John Gottman," *Amazon*, https://www.amazon.com/John-Gottman/e/B002H0RGGoXA%3Fref=dbs_a_mng_rwt_scns_share.

[4] John Gottman, *Why Marriages Succeed or Fail: And How You Can Make Yours Last* (New York: Simon and Schuster, 1995), 68-102.

[5] John Gottman, *The Marriage Clinic: A Scientifically-Based Marital Therapy* (New York: W.W. Norton, 1999), 128.

anger. I see it as anger in one of its deepest forms. It shows itself in bitterness or despising another or something.

The Hidden Power of Contempt

One definition of *contempt* is "disregard for something that should be taken into account."[6] When a person is given a subpoena to appear in court and disregards that summons, he or she may be headed for a headache of a wake-up call. The legal system is not something to play with or take lightly because its extensive power can hit you where it hurts—from incarceration to the pocketbook in fines and fees. No less serious is the mate who disregards the interests, feelings, desires, aspirations, and dreams within one's spouse—things partners should always consider and take into account about each other throughout a marriage.

Treating something or someone with contempt has another aspect or side to it. As with most words in the dictionary, this word has multiple or secondary meanings. Another definition of *contempt* is "a feeling that a person or thing is beneath one's dignity and unworthy of one's notice, respect, or concern."[7] This additional perspective of contempt can promote a spirit of bitterness, not only in the perpetrator of contempt but also reactively and more pronounced within the one receiving scorn or feeling disregarded as a spouse. If enough slights are allowed to add up, it may prove to be a recipe for divorce, whether legal or virtual.

What do I mean by virtual divorce? Not all divorces are of the paper variety or played out legally in a courtroom. Many divorces are virtual, meaning psychological, emotional, or

---

[6] "Contempt," *Oxford University Press*, https://www.lexico.com/en/definition/contempt.

[7] Random House Kernerman Webster's College Dictionary, © 2010 K Dictionaries Ltd. Copyright 2005, 1997, 1991 by Random House, Inc. All rights reserved.

physical separation. In such cases, an emotionally battered or deprived spouse may withdraw from a partner in every way but the legal one. This can often result when a spouse (or both) fails to do his or her part in loving and caring for the other spouse, as the Bible calls marriage partners to do. And ultimately, a court of law may be called upon by a spouse or both to turn a virtual divorce into a legal one, which strikes the final blow to a marriage by officially dissolving the union.

Love Turns Sour

We find an account in the Bible that illustrates this principle of contempt. It is a love story that has gone sour. Michal's father, King Saul, faced a major threat. The invading Philistine army had a giant named Goliath, who stood six and a half cubits plus a span tall. There is some uncertainty around the exact length of an ancient cubit; therefore, estimations of Goliath's height range from six feet six inches to around eleven feet tall.[8] For three days, the giant called out and challenged any Israelite to come forth and fight him (See 1 Samuel 17). None answered the call, for all of Israel's army was afraid of and greatly dismayed at this giant, until a young Jewish shepherd named David stepped forth and volunteered.

Now Michal, Saul's daughter, loved David (See 1 Samuel 18:20).

Long story short, David won his battle against Goliath. "David Saves the Kingdom!" may have been the next day's headline in *The Jerusalem Post*. In addition to David's prowess on the battlefield, he also was a skilled harpist and a prolific psalmist. The Bible further

---

[8] Joel Ryan, "How Tall Was Goliath and What Do We Really Know About Him?" *The Crosswalk Devotional*, May 18, 2021, https://www.crosswalk.com/faith/bible-study/how-tall-was-goliath-what-do-we-really-know-about-goliath.html.

records his exploits as a shepherd guarding his sheep. He single-handedly killed both a bear and a lion while defending the sheep. No wonder Michal was smitten. This young man could do it all.

But then a problem surfaced. Michal had a jealous dad, who happened to be a king. Her father, King Saul, became so concerned over David's rising popularity due to his exploits that he perceived David as a future threat to his throne. To keep a close eye on David, Saul gave his daughter to be married to David. But Saul was determined that David would have to be eliminated, and he plotted to do so. Daughter Michal got wind of her father's plot. Through her counterplot, David escaped under the stealth of darkness.

Let's fast-forward nineteen chapters and some eighteen-to-twenty years later, and David is now King. "Then it happened as the ark of the LORD came into the city of David that Michal the daughter of Saul looked out the window and saw King David leaping and dancing before the LORD; and *she despised him in her heart*" (2 Samuel 6:16, emphasis is mine).

Where Did Love Go?

What happened? Where did Michal's love go? And did David actually love her? What put a chink in the knight-in-shining-armor persona Michal originally saw as love? We find possible clues about the expressed love. It was displaced by disdain, which settled deep into Michal's heart and eyes. The dancing and exuberance that David showed toward his God when he entered Jerusalem after leading his army to victory may have made her jealous. Did she resent David's great love and public show for his God while giving her scant attention? After all, she remained childless throughout what perhaps was a loveless marriage with David.

If you track the eighteen-to-twenty-year period that spanned the books of 1 and 2 Samuel, which chronicled David and Michal's relationship, other factors may also have led to Michal's disdain. First, in addition to engaging in multiple marriages after being separated from Michal and fathering many children, David never returned to claim his first love after she had put her life at risk while helping him escape her father.

Although it was common for men of that day to have multiple marriages, that practice may not have lessened the pain in Michal's feelings of abandonment and betrayal. The brave warrior that she thought David to be was nowhere to be found. You can imagine her thinking, *I am his love, his first love, his wife. He is my husband! Where is he? Why isn't he coming for me?* We have no record of this brave, fearless warrior attempting to return, rescue, and then reclaim her. Some might suggest David desired to honor God by respecting Saul's kingship, which would have kept David from returning with force. But David didn't have to return and fight a battle; a little stealth to reclaim his wife would have sufficed.

Second, over time while living in her father's kingdom, her father gave her to be married to another man. Eventually, her father died, and his son took over the throne. David's warriors came against the son, and the overmatched son made overtures for peace. David accepted on one condition. He demanded, and he was granted the return of Michal. While David's soldiers brought Michal back to David, her current husband ran alongside the cart she was riding in, cried, and pleaded for them not to take his wife. David was not even there to claim her. Members of his army brought her back. Did she feel as loved by David as she had by the husband who ran alongside the ones taking her while pleading to keep her? In comparison, did she feel she was nothing more than chattel to David?

Third, since David was not even there while Michal was being returned, Michal was not asked what *she* wanted. Even though women were often viewed and treated as chattel in that day, the view did not necessarily negate those husbands who loved and cared for their wives. In other words, I doubt every husband treated his wife as if he owned her. The actions of Michal's husband appeared to show that he deeply loved her: He pleaded with King David's men not to take her. If her current husband saw her as chattel, he likely would have reasoned that he could purchase another. He could have bartered a business deal to get something in return for her. Seeing his wife as chattel doesn't seem to fit the tenor of a husband pleading to keep his wife.

In the end, the love story between David and Michal is a sad one. It offers the reader lessons about love relationships and the way they can go sour if one or both parties do not nurture and hold them in high esteem.

The Means to a Fulfilling Marriage

As you examine yourself in the mirror of marriage, do you see any developing or ongoing signs of your spouse acting against you or of you acting against your spouse that should cause concern in this area of contempt? Do you or your spouse appear to be pulling away from the other mentally, emotionally, physically, or spiritually? Have you noticed any sharpness developing in your spouse's tone or your tone when you interact? Is there any body language by your spouse or you that causes (or should cause) concern? Have you or your spouse prioritized togetherness? Do you still display affection as partners, or is it a thing of the past? Ask yourself how you might be contributing to any negativity within your marriage relationship and resolve to clean up those areas that you are responsible for.

It may be a fatal flaw in marriage to assume that a mate will continue to love a spouse who disregards everything that makes a mate who he or she is. When marriage is chronically about one spouse more than it is the other, the selfish spouse will likely end up with a distant, cold, and uncaring mate. A fulfilling marriage experience must be equally inclusive of both spouses. Anything less may cost the offending party dearly and lead to the forfeiture of any hope to experience marriage as God intended it to be. The exercise in the next chapter will prove critical in providing the direction, answers, and hope you need to get your marriage on a positive course, whether you are the perpetrator or the recipient of contempt in the marriage.

CHAPTER 3

The Exercise

IN MY MARRIAGE, I WANTED a peaceful home and a happy togetherness. I wanted a contented wife who accepted me for who and how I was, for I saw myself as a decent guy whom my wife ought to be thankful she had (Little did I realize how not nice I could be that marriage exposed). Conversely, my wife wanted much of the same things for herself. We both wanted to enjoy life, but I thought she was blocking my happiness. I reasoned that I had little to do with our marital discord. Needless to say, but I'll say it anyway, I was proven wrong.

I did not feel like I came into marriage with an anger issue, so any anger issues in me that surfaced in the early years of our marriage had to be due to her. I would tell her, "I never got angry before I married you." Growing tired of hearing that wearisome refrain during another round of my venting, she offered a rebuttal with an insightful comment. She said, "Jim, do you know why you never got angry before you married me? Because you would always walk away from conflict and never had to face it. You told me so yourself. You avoided all conflict." She was correct in her assessment.

Face the Issues

By first acknowledging the wise words that marriage doesn't create problems but reveals them and then applying biblical truths to a willing heart, I began engaging in shedding my pattern of avoidance. I quit placing blame on my wife. I learned to talk and walk through resolving conflict. I began to own my shortcomings and focus on learning to master myself. That mastery manifested itself through character growth and resulted in the development of a healthy and successful marriage.

As both Joni and I focused on conceding control to the Lord and worked on ourselves, we learned how to enjoy marriage as God intended it to be. You may be asking, *But how does one do that?* We will head there next.

I have identified seventy-nine of the most repetitive and damaging problem areas culled from the lives of counselees who have brought their marital issues and discord before me as a counselor. Also included in the list are problem areas my wife and I faced. I encourage you to engage in this exercise and see what you learn during this self-evaluation. Before you and the list meet, I want to give you some words of caution and detailed instructions on how to engage the list.

First, here are some words of caution. This list and the exercise I'm about to propose to you are the teeth of the book. Handle this exercise carefully, as this can have a bite to it. It will not be easy to look into the mirror of marriage and see parts of yourself revealed. I have used this exercise for years with individuals and couples during marriage counseling and in my own marriage, along with employing this exercise in family and individual counseling. No other counseling efforts or strategies that I have encountered or employed have compared to the counseling success I've seen recipients enjoy when engaging and committing to what this exercise entails.

Second, before seeing the list, read these instructions for the exercise.

1. Identify the problem areas that *you* bring to the marriage by circling the words that apply to you. The words you circle should reflect a consistent problem or pattern and not a problem that surfaces every-once-in-a-while (unless such a problem is especially egregious, such as infidelity).
2. Of the problems you circle, identify your top three problems by putting a star next to them.

For the next part of this exercise, some further words of caution are in order.

> Do *not* engage in steps three, four, and five if you or your spouse cannot handle constructive criticism; otherwise, this part of the exercise could lead to damaging arguments.

Obviously, I am not physically present with you and your spouse to oversee this exercise, for if I were, I could endeavor to mitigate or defuse any potentially negative reactions between you and your spouse that might occur while engaging in this part of the exercise. However, this exercise will prove to be extremely valuable and necessary in helping the interested reader's search for a better marriage. You, as the reader, must determine if you should engage your spouse in points three, four, and five of this exercise.

If your spouse chooses to join you in this exercise, both should complete steps one and two and then proceed.

1. Once you have completed the process of circling your problem areas, per instructions in steps one and two, exchange your list with your spouse. Put a check mark

on your spouse's paper next to each problem you believe your spouse missed (did not circle), but is a problem area that you see in your spouse. Have your spouse do the same with your list of problem areas you bring to the marriage.

2. On your spouse's list, put an asterisk next to the top three problem areas you believe your spouse brings to the marriage. Have your spouse do the same with your problem areas that he sees in you.

3. Return the list to the original owner and take time to review and digest your spouse's perspective of you as noted on your list.

When I have conducted this exercise with married couples in my office, the responses to a partner's input were quite telling. Flinching heads and raised eyebrows led to comments such as, "Really?" "That's *not* me!" "No way," "I can't believe you think that," "Is that how you see me?" "I'm surprised," "I'm shocked!" and "I'm hurt you think that." On rare occasions, I have heard, "I agree; I can see that in me."

You might be thinking, *If the book is about seeing myself in the mirror of marriage, why bring in a mate's view?* Because when two people marry, two become one flesh. When you look into that mirror of marriage, your partner will also be within the mirror's frame. Living together as one in the most intimate commitment, your spouse's input is valuable in assessing the problem areas you might have brought into the marriage, may still exhibit, and as of yet do not see. But here's a caveat: Just because your spouse believes certain things to be true about you and your problem areas does not mean he or she is accurate in the assessment, nor does it mean his or her view of you is automatically invalid because you disagree.

This is why couples must identify and talk through perspectives and differences. The genesis of talking things through first requires issues to be identified. What are the problem areas each brings to the marriage? Is each spouse's view of himself or herself and the other spouse an accurate depiction of truth and reality? In my experience, this exercise does an excellent job of promoting evaluation and dialogue, which can benefit each spouse in making a positive marriage connection. Now we come to the list.

Marriage Doesn't Create Problems; It Reveals Problems

This list is a compilation over the years of the most repetitive and damaging problem areas brought up by counselees during my counseling sessions with them.

Identify the problem areas you bring to the marriage by circling the appropriate words

Critical	Self-Centered	Avoider	Worldly	Poor Self-Image	Passive-Aggressive
Lying	Too Dependent	Prideful	Negative	Wishy-Washy	Conflict Averse
Angry	Demeaning	Stubborn	Vengeful	Inconsistent	Stonewalling
Lazy	Unforgiving	Defensive	Interrupts	Acidic Tongue	Too Sensitive
Jealous	Independent	*Depression	Talker	Hard on Oneself	Gaslights
Moody	Inconsiderate	*Bipolar	Anxious	Perfectionist	Not Affectionate
Yelling	Controlling	Insecure	Type A	Manipulative	Addictive Personality
Enabler	Judgmental	Impatient	Appeaser	Demanding	Jump to Conclusions
In Debt	Inflexible	Withdrawn	Idealistic	Too Direct	Strong-Willed
Non-talker	Internalizes	Exaggerates	Sugarcoats	Romanticizes	Procrastinates
Covert	Resentful	Bossy	Narcissistic	Irresponsible	Workaholic
Guilty	Indecisive	Obsessive	Intense	Double-standard	Confrontational
Frustration	Infidelity	Trust Issues	Temper	Sexual Matters	Bitter
Histrionics (Dramatic)		Other?			

- In many cases, this may prove to be a physiological problem, not of your own making. But it identifies as a problem area if you are irresponsible in managing your health care.

Once you have completed this exercise and walked through the results, make a plan for improvement. If your spouse joined you in the exercise, that's great. Now you can plan together. But if your spouse did not participate in this exercise, you'll need to go it alone in planning changes for yourself, which still may result in a positive yield for your marriage.

- What issues did you identify about yourself that need work and change?
- How will you go about bringing change to those problem areas that affect and afflict your relationship with your spouse?
- If both spouses participated, what did you learn from the other person's perspective – about him or herself, and about you?

Whatever problem areas you identified about yourself, there are resources available to help in your resolution or at the least, mitigation of those problem areas. If you have a computer and basic skills in using one, you can google sites that offer suggestions and plans on ways to overcome specific personal shortcomings, which left untreated can become problem areas in your marriage. For example, if you have an anger problem, do an internet search by typing in "how to handle anger" or similar words. If the computer path is not for you, make a counseling appointment with a church pastor or a counselor. Visit a bookstore and purchase salient material that addresses your shortcomings. Use a Bible concordance and study Bible passages under the headings you need. Whatever you do, guard against just trying harder within yourself. That usually doesn't work. Plan your work and then work your plan to bring about a better you.

If despite all your concerted efforts to become a better you and make your marriage work or work better and things have not changed, rest assured that you can do nothing more to make your marriage work or save it, if it proves irretrievable. Your efforts in positive personal change concerning your shortcomings will not go to waste or be for naught; but rather, those efforts will go a long way in helping you move forward positively in whatever direction you may find yourself going.

You might wonder why I highlighted the differences that divide a couple and the problems each brings rather than focusing on things that are alike and strengths that link couples together. As you read through the book, I believe this question will be more fully answered, but I will also briefly answer it here. Personal traits that link a couple together are what originally attracted you and your mate to each other. You *didn't* see those underlying shortcomings that could divide you if those things are allowed to become prominent in your relationship. If the focus would stay on the positive parts of each spouse, then those mutual traits would greatly help overshadow problem areas and provide a link to a happy and successful marriage, but keeping the correct focus is a challenge that many spouses fail to do, hence we must deal with the reality that shortcomings and foibles play in threatening a marriage.

Far too often, the differences that divide—when eventually allowed to take center stage in a marriage and permitted to become too large or prominent for the other spouse to ignore—will outweigh or shade the good traits that originally linked a couple together. At that point, the differences cannot be swept under the rug, but they must be dealt with—front and center. And I have found that a couple's problems allowed to take center stage happens more times than not.

CHAPTER 4

Confessions of a Married Man (and Woman)

WHAT WOULD I HAVE IDENTIFIED about myself in the early years of my marriage if I had done the exercise in chapter three? In addition to being an avoider, I brought the following problem areas into my marriage: I was stubborn, a non-talker when emotionally hurt, inconsiderate, too sensitive, and unforgiving, among other things. I showed some aspects of gaslighting.[9] In my defense, I did not gaslight in the full sense of the word, for I did not intentionally engage in this practice, which I believe is a major component in the original etymology of the term.[10] However, the damage could be just as bad whether it's intentional or not.

At times in my thinking (and wrongly so), I was framing my wife with my supportive facts, indicating that she was the key

---

[9] This is a psychological manipulation of a person, usually over an extended period, which causes the victim to question the validity of his or her own thoughts, perception of reality, or memories and typically leads to confusion, loss of confidence and self-esteem, uncertainty of his or her emotional or mental stability, and a dependency on the perpetrator. "Gaslighting," *Merriam-Webster. com Dictionary*, https://www.merriam-webster.com/dictionary/gaslighting.

[10] Dr. Oliver Tearle, "The Curious Origin of the Word Gaslighting," *Synonymuse: The Writers Thesaurus*, https://synonymuse.com/gaslighting-word-origin/.

source of our marital problems. Although she contributed her fair share of problems to the marriage, as did I, she was in no way the sole or primary source of our struggles. I incorrectly created an unbalanced picture of our life together, with her cast as the one (the villain?) who contributed more to our marital struggles.

During my formative, childhood years and into my teenage years, if anyone emotionally hurt me, and it was repeated enough times, I withdrew and reached the place of no return with them. It was part of my sidestepping and avoiding conflict. I mentally wrote the offenders off from my life. When others crossed my line, there was little those people could do to get back into my good graces. I just wanted to sidestep them and move on. Imagine how that played out in a marriage.

A Reality Check

Because I was a Christian, and now a married man, by God's grace marriage awakened me to the need to work on myself instead of working on my wife. I have continually worked on the problems within myself. For the most part, I have banished them from the home. I say for the most part because the temptation to fall back into any destructive former way or mindset can (and does) rear its ugly head at any time. I must remain vigilant if I want ongoing victory in my life. This potential for regression is likely in all of us. Consider the Bible's warnings and directives.

> Therefore let him who thinks he stands take heed that he does not fall. (1 Corinthians 10:12)

> In reference to your former manner of life, you lay aside the old self, which is being corrupted in accordance with the lusts of deceit, and that you be renewed in the spirit of your mind, and put on the new self, which in the likeness of God has

been created in righteousness and holiness of the truth. (Ephesians 4:22–24)

My wife's list that described her problem areas within the marriage was as long as mine was. A problem area for her was her romantic illusion of marriage. To some, such a problem would seem quite harmless. To what extent could romantic illusions cause damage? Joni thought that within a short time of being married, any marital issues that we needed to resolve would be minuscule and few and that in short order, they would work themselves out. After all, she reasoned that we were in love and that surely our love would settle us into wedded bliss.

Unknowingly, Joni set herself up for disillusionment and disappointment of the Disneyland variety. It didn't take long for her to learn that marriage doesn't unfold that way, and that revelation was discouraging to her. Fifty-plus years later and now possessing a realistic and holistic view of marriage, yet you will find her watching and enjoying one of her favorite channels—the Hallmark Channel. The programming is known for its happily-ever-after, romantic narratives and a plethora of heartwarming, seasonal (Thanksgiving and Christmas) stories. She loves to watch those shows because she still embodies and enjoys that happily-ever-after feeling in life. But her dreams and perspectives are grounded in knowing, understanding, and accepting that both joys and trials (and human failure) are part of marriage in a fallen world—even Christian marriages – yet happiness can still be achieved.

The Death of a Dream

As we all learn, reality works differently than fantasy does. In the 1990s, the Disney empire developed and built its own town in Florida named Celebration. It was a town that should have been as close to heaven on Earth as you could get, celebrating the best of living conditions, and populated by what they hoped were some of the best people they could draw to its community. After all, the town to be built would be fashioned by the same mindset that envisioned and constructed Disneyland and later Disney World. At the dedication of Disneyland on July 17, 1955, Walt Disney said,

> To all who come to this happy place: welcome. Disneyland is your land. Here age relives fond memories of the past … and here youth may savor the challenge and promise of the future. Disneyland is dedicated to the ideals, the dreams and the hard facts which have created America … with the hope that it will be a source of joy and inspiration to all the world.

Some fourteen years after the town's inception, one news headline read, "How the Disney Dream Died in Celebration." [11] The article reported on the first murder in the community, followed by a man dying in a shootout with police. Then there were residents not following through in maintaining their part in upkeep of the community. But there were those still putting a positive spin on their community by reasoning, as one resident noted, "One murder in fourteen years? Where can you go on the entire planet and find this kind of statistic? Tell me." [12]

The article then spoke of a lesser-known fact: Walt Disney sought total control over this town's inception and working parts by creating his own government, thus assuring the success of

---

[11] Ed Pilkington, "How the Disney Dream Died in Celebration," *The Guardian,* December 13, 2010, https://www.theguardian.com/world/2010/dec/13/celebration-death-of-a-dream.

[12] Ed Pilkington, "How the Disney Dream Died in Celebration," *The Guardian,* December 13, 2010, https://www.theguardian.com/world/2010/dec/13/celebration-death-of-a-dream.

his vison and dream of community bliss. Amazingly, the local authorities granted him the power to run his own government! He had the power to raise taxes while also controlling all public amenities. Yet all that control did not result in what he had envisioned. Likewise, marriage does not work as you may first envision, no matter how much control you have, or you might think you have, or you want to have, in being able to determine the desired outcome.

People have problems, and they bring those problems into marriage, no matter where you live, who you are, or whom you marry. You cannot escape yourself. You must first deal with yourself. As benign as the fairy-tale dream of happily ever after may appear to be, there is the danger of never learning to deal with foibles and fault lines that couples must face in each self, and in each other, to be addressed as part of a successful, happy, and lasting marriage. We are multilayered people. One could spend countless hours trying to separate the layers that have made us or our mates what and who we are. But far more important is what we do with what and who we discover ourselves to be and where we go from here. Honest assessment, correction, and moving forward offer the best hope for solving problems within ourselves and our marriages.

Assessing and Addressing

My wife and I have had our internal battles. I mentioned earlier in the book about my struggle with being forgiving. My wife has always been quick to forgive, but I have had to work through forgiveness. She could not understand why it was so hard for me to forgive, and I could not comprehend how it appeared so easy for her to forgive. Fortunately, she has always remained quick to forgive, and her model, along with the influence of the holy scriptures on my life, has nudged me over to that winning way of life and marriage. Her example was and is a living model of how good and right can triumph. If we are open to being changed from people who can be damaging to another, to becoming people who are positive marriage partners, we'll reap the benefits of our concerted efforts. Too often in marriage, we rub our bad traits onto and into each other as mates, by lowering ourselves to fighting fire with fire with each other, in which no one profits, but all eventually lose.

Early in our marriage, my wife's behavior was passive-aggressive. She would be passive (calm) in her demeanor and character, which would look good on the surface. But underneath, certain things in our marriage churned within her to the point that she would work at trying to have me see things her way, which she deemed was the right way. That's not her penchant today. Her change happened largely when I overcame the very thing that triggered such behavior in her: my stubborn adherence to *my* way being the so-called right way.

When I made my leadership style more approachable and inclusive, I felt better because her pushback against my leadership subsided significantly. I became accountable as the leader of us and not just my spouse. She feels, and is, a partner in that leadership. I learned to lead the biblical way: a call by God for husbands to lead by modeling the message of servanthood, sacrifice, and humility, which equate to love. Many husbands I have counseled see leadership as getting to call the shots and always having the last word. Such a mindset is not God's intent for a Christian husband.

When Joni and I faced our individual selves, we began working on ourselves instead of each other. Even to this day, the list idea continues to help us. At sporadic times throughout the year, I pull out the list of seventy-nine problem areas, which I describe in chapter three, or I'll pull out the "Twenty-Five *A*s in an Awesome Marriage" (Appendix 1) so that Joni and I can engage the lists and evaluate ourselves. The reason we have made this an intentional practice is so that we will diligently continue to work on ourselves. We deal with any slipups, for slipups that are allowed to grow can soon become habits that may turn chronic and then toxic.

The last time we pulled out the list of seventy-nine problem areas, I was hopefully confident that I would fare well. At our stage of life and with the effort we had put into our marriage, we should not have many wrongs to circle. As I perused the list of seventy-nine problem areas, I did not identify any resurfacing or new problem areas when evaluating myself or my wife, but from the corner of my eye, I saw her circling something. I was curious. Did she circle something about herself that needed correction or about me? When we both finished, I quickly gave her my evaluation of myself and of her (no noticeable slipups or issues concerning either of us). I was anxious to get her evaluation and see what she had circled from the list. She had circled one area about me: inconsiderate.

I went into quiz mode. "Inconsiderate? Wow, I'm surprised. Haven't you noticed that when I am home, and I see you arrive home from grocery shopping, I hurry out to carry in the groceries? I faithfully continue to open doors for you and walk by your side (and not ten paces ahead of you!), and I make sure we share the TV remote, and I put my dirty dishes in the dishwasher and not on the counter, as I used to do." Now it was time to find out the why of what she had identified. This confession is embarrassing for me, but it's worth sharing if it helps your marriage.

Her reply was, "Do you remember several weeks ago when we hosted a get-together of our friends?"

"Yes," I responded.

"Before our guests arrived, do you remember sticking your fork in the serving pot?" she asked.

I thought for a moment and then answered, "Yes," but I was wondering, *Where is she going with this?*

Then came her coup de grâce. "After you put the fork in your mouth, you took the same fork and went back for more. If any of our guests saw that, do you think they would want to take something from that serving pot?"

Ouch. Stick a fork in me because I was done. After a few defensive maneuvers, I gave it up and acknowledged that what I did *was* inconsiderate. One of the old problems from my early years had resurfaced (I also used to drink directly out of the milk carton).

It's important to note the way that my wife approached me when I had my slipup with the fork and the serving pot. She was calm, respectful, and measured. She did not read me the riot act, have an edge to her voice, or belabor her point. That positive conduct went a long way in assuaging potential conflict. My willingness to be vulnerable in my marriage relationship was also helpful. It opened me up, and I invited my wife to speak into my life.

I am quick to add that no one's marriage is perfect, and neither is ours. This most recent example of going over the list showed no falling back on her conduct and revealed one setback on my part. Sometimes we fall back into problem areas and need to correct ourselves. Even after fifty-plus years of marriage, my wife and I remain a work in progress. My wife and I are not aiming for the impossible (perfection), but our aim is to love in a way that the other sees and feels mutual respect, fueled by continual effort.

As you look into the mirror of marriage, linger awhile. Pause. Gaze deeply. What do you see? What confessions and concessions will you make about yourself that you may have been overlooking or dismissive of because you were focusing on your spouse's wrongs and not on yourself? Does your spouse have wrongs you could point out? Surely, and we'll get there in our consideration of those foibles, but let's first do a thorough self-evaluation. Jot down the discoveries you have made about yourself and will now acknowledge. Now, write down what you will do with these revelations. Will you keep them to yourself or address them with your spouse, so he or she can be encouraged in knowing that "you get it." It is a spirit of accountability that can help heal and strengthen a marriage.

Whatever the marriage needs are, seeing yourself in the mirror of marriage is a major step in the process of marital growth. Recognition, confession, consideration, and change are four major building blocks in a winning marriage. They are key components in the love equation.

CHAPTER 5

Dangerous Intersections

A SIGN WARNS OF A dangerous intersection ahead, reading, "proceed with caution." Flashing yellow lights may be attached to the sign, enhancing the call for alertness. Seasoned drivers know well just how dangerous various intersections can be. This may not be so true for most novices in the driver's seat.

I taught my five daughters how to drive. Somewhat complicating matters was my determination that each of them would learn how to drive a stick shift, also known as a manual transmission. It was quite the experience to have my in-training daughters drive up to an intersection on a hill with a stop sign, and me in the passenger seat. Being stopped at an intersection on an incline with a novice driver operating a stick shift was not a stress-free environment for me. But I survived it all, and through the experiences, I have a lot of humorous stories and memories to recall and enjoy.

Let's apply the above illustration to marriage. Training my daughters to drive took place in a suburban setting and not in a city environment. I liken suburban driving to interacting with everyday relationships with people. But the marriage relationship is more like encountering intersections in city driving (Think of New York City, where I have driven many times). When entering those intersections, you better up your game and be constantly alert to your surroundings. Behind the wheel in your car, your eyes will need to dart from the traffic signal to posted signs, which give a host of instructions, and also to crosswalks that may be active with pedestrians, baby strollers, or bicycles. Fast-approaching emergency vehicles can rush through intersections at any moment. Added to the stress are the actions of surrounding motorists. All parts of a busy city intersection call for caution, alertness, and attention. Letting your guard down as a driver – even for a few seconds – can result in unforeseen and regrettable consequences.

Foolish husbands believe the marriage experience is very simple: "Just do as I say and think, and stay off my back, and we'll be happy." For many wives it's a matter of "love me and listen to me, and we'll be happy." But like a busy city intersection, navigating marriage is not a simple or stress free matter, for marriage has many moving parts. The personalities, tastes, experiences, preferences, fears, joys, pain, moods, disappointments, aspirations, and dreams of two individuals merge daily at intersecting points in everyday life. Awareness, alertness, caution, concern, and care are all components that each spouse needs to bring to marriage intersections. If you don't have these traits, you would be wise to acquire them.

At this point we'll shift focus beyond examining primarily ourselves in marriage to mixing into view our spouse and how that spouse is part of the marital relationship. We'll investigate myriad intersections and interactions within a marriage.

Navigation Details—Setting Your GPS

While each spouse works on personal changes, those changes do not happen overnight. Married couples can find themselves living together virtually 24-7, week after week, month after month, and year after year—for decades! How does a couple successfully navigate the day-to-day intersections in marriage while each spouse also endeavors to identify and work on personal issues? Entering busy traffic intersections is not the time for carefree or careless driving, and successful marriages aren't filled with carefree and careless living.

In marriage, attention to detail is frequently overlooked, but such attention is a prerequisite in thriving marriages. Chronic carelessness and inattention regarding one's spouse or oneself may cost your connection to him or her and eventually the loss of your marriage. At the very least, it will cost you the loss of joy in your marriage.

To experience marriage as it ought to be, a couple needs to be thoughtful toward each other while learning to merge their two lives into one. Within marriages, opportunities for crashes and clashes are plentiful when the lives and paths of husbands and wives intersect in marriage.

In addition to the varied issues that surface in marriage, consider how each person's actions, reactions, or inaction affect the other. Money, trust, medical issues, debt, spending and personal habits, hygiene, friends, priorities, hobbies, loss of a child, laziness, child-rearing, relatives, in-laws, values, choices, chores, quirks, addictions, differences of opinion, religion, dreams, personality traits, jealousies, disappointments, and hurt are some of the things that need to be safely and wisely navigated during ongoing marital travel. Let's face it, with that many items or issues confronting a couple, there will be disagreements, arguments, and fights. There will be differing points of view, moody moments, real or perceived slights and hurts, and major setbacks and losses—you name it. Issues that surface will range from the trite, silly, and foolish to the hot, heavy, and relationship-altering.

Since arguments are a given in any marriage, we ought to consider some ground rules to make fighting fair. Low blows are not permitted. Both partners have an equal shot at speaking their piece while respectfully hearing from the other. I have fashioned together the following twenty-two rules that make for a fair fight in marriage, which in turn, make problem resolution more attainable. This benefits both parties. Some may argue that twenty-two rules are about twelve too many; after all, God gave only Ten Commandments in the Bible.

Some would suggest three or four rules at the most. They reason that the fewer the rules, the easier it would be to remember, especially when two people are in an argument. Who will remember a list of rules in the heat of battle? However, I have found every one of these rules is vital and necessary to know, remember, and employ. How you choose to do that is up to you, but I believe your marriage will benefit greatly if you learn to incorporate the insights from everything on this list.

Twenty-Two Rules for Fighting Fair

1. No Sweeping Generalities

This means not using words or phrases such as "You never" or "You always." Is it true that your mate sometimes fails to do what he or she should do, such as helping? Yes, it's true. Have there been times when your mate did something he or she should not have done? Yes. But painting with broad strokes will discourage your mate when you say something like, "You never help." This becomes especially egregious when your accused spouse can think of specific times and ways that he or she *has* helped in the past— even going out of his or her way to do so. This attack will cause your mate to recoil and think, *Why ever help again? My spouse doesn't ever notice or appreciate when I do help. Forget it.*

2. No Pejorative Language

Don't use put-downs, for all such words do is belittle. Words such as, "You're just like your mother [or father]," "You can't do anything right," or "You'll never change." To negatively compare your mate to anyone is asking for trouble, and you will surely find it, either in a blowup or a clam up by your spouse. Put-downs by a spouse often beget put-downs by the partner.

Especially painful to a spouse is when a partner's spoken put-down involves a spouse's family of origin. A spouse has the latitude to criticize his or her family of origin, but the better rule of thumb is for *you* as the partner not to bad-mouth your in-laws. However, you will need to show support for your spouse if he or she is battling damaging parental or family influence directed his or her way. But be very careful in what you say about your spouse's family and how you say it.

3. No Patronizing

Don't treat your spouse with feigned kindness while portraying a feeling of superiority and saying, "Sure, whatever you say," "I'm sure you're always right," or "I know you're never wrong." It's you getting in a dig that you know will irritate your spouse when your spouse is trying to make a point. Also, keep in mind that words are not the only way to patronize. It can also be done with nonverbal gestures, such as a fake smile or a rolling of the eyes.

4. Stay on Point

Do not bring up other issues that cloud clarity while discussing the subject. Couples can wrongly bring up past scenarios that do nothing but muddy the waters. In wrongly doing so, it does not take long until both of you are off point in what is being discussed, and the initial focus becomes lost.

5. No Raised Voices

It is easier said than done, but fighting fair is about learning to control yourself. Make it a point to agree that raised voices call for a pause to reset emotions. Unfortunately, there can be disagreement on whether a voice is being raised or not. The rule of thumb is this: Be accountable to the spouse who is sensitive to hearing a voice raised.

I have witnessed arguments between spouses whom I have counseled where one spouse appeared to be getting heated. When I called this spouse on it, I was told, "This is how I grew up. This is how we would talk to each other in our family, and no one was mad." In such cases, one must remember that spouses are in a *new* family now, where ground rules and actions may call for different dynamics. You must take a different person into account. Your spouse may have grown up in an environment that is opposite to yours, so you must establish new ground rules that you both understand and accept.

Here is a hint. Shed the standby excuses that say, "But I'm [ethnicity], and that's how we talk," if the issue is loudness, or "That's the [ethnicity] in me," if the issue is stubbornness. Christian culture is well explained in the Bible. If you claim to be a Christian, you should concede and adhere to that culture. Any responses and reactions should reflect the reality that projects a spirit that says, "That's the Christian in me."

6. Give Attention to What Each Spouse Says

In a heated battle, we can become so defensive that our minds go into immediate response mode to counter whatever we immediately sense our spouses are beginning to lay on us. We hear only the beginning of what someone is saying that triggers us into formulating our response to what *we* want to say rather than listening to the whole of what he or she is saying.

7. No Mind Reading

"I know what you're thinking." "I know why you did that." If you want to shut down a discussion quickly and close your spouse's mind to further discussion, simply tell your spouse what he or she is thinking and feeling and the reason for those thoughts and feelings. The shutdown can be immediate. No one likes a person presumptively telling another what that other person is thinking, feeling, or wanting during an argument.

8. Seek Understanding

Use words like, "What I hear you saying is," or "What is coming across to me is." Much understanding is crippled because what one spouse hears is not what the other spouse said or meant. Seeking clarification plays a major role in reducing arguments and promoting resolutions, for many arguments form when information is passed through an inaccurate grid in a person's mind. Clarification promotes understanding.

9. No Interrupting

When you interrupt, you are often not listening. Interrupting breaks your spouse's train of thought and looks like an act of rudeness to the one who is interrupted. The one who interrupts is more interested in sharing his or her mind than listening to a spouse's complete thoughts.

10. No Dominating the Conversation

One way a spouse will avoid arguing is to clam up because arguing is stressful and unsettling. This can easily lead to the more aggressive spouse taking and keeping the floor in an argument. This means any so-called discussion ends up being a one-way street. Fighting fairly means that the more dominant mate can recognize the need for equal expression. He or she will pull back while at the same time drawing out the more hesitant spouse. The hesitant spouse must be willing to speak up so that conversation can occur yet feel assured the more dominant spouse will not attack what is being said once the hesitant spouse speaks up.

11. No Assumptions

Many arguments form around situations or activities that occur when things are left unshared, not planned together, or not talked through with a spouse so that both can be on the same page of understanding. Getting a couple (and a family) on the same page will keep self-inflicted disruptions of plans at a minimum.

For example, the family is planning to leave on vacation tomorrow, but the time of departure was not discussed. It was only assumed. The next day, the wife's understood responsibility is to have the family packed and ready to leave by noon (in her thinking). At the same time, the husband stays at his job until late afternoon before coming home. With the travel destination only three hours away, he assumes that he can get in a day's worth of work, with the family departing after dinner for their destination. The wife assumes noon is the departure time. She is none too happy when he returns home, but he is upbeat and ready to roll, having assumed that all is going according to plan. The vacation is already starting on the wrong foot. Herein lies the potential for a tainted or ruined vacation.

12. No Bullying

This especially applies to men because they can be more intimidating due to their sizes or voices. Wives can also be guilty of bullying and intimidating by using their attitudes, anger, or tongues against more placid husbands. If a husband and wife constantly go *mano a mano* with each other, the arguments may prove to be both brutal and destructive to the marriage. Standing toe-to-toe while arguing with your spouse and no holds barred may leave you feeling satisfied that you made your point and that you didn't back down. But over time, you will learn that you won many battles but eventually lost the war (and your marriage).

13. Be Conscious of Nonverbal Communication

We speak with far more than our words when we communicate. Damaging body language that emanates from our spirits can clearly be seen in eye-rolling, slight headshakes, smirks, half-smiles, a posture that shows impatience or disinterest, shoulder shrugs, and frowning. These expressions are noticed by a spouse during interaction. Such displays that we show to our spouse will discourage him or her from continuing in discussion, hinder any desire for future discussions, and give rise to a spirit of contempt.

14. No Use of the *D* Word

When arguing, a spouse may choose to go for the jugular and raise the alarm in a partner or try to gain the upper hand in an argument by striking fear into the listening partner. The *D* word is divorce. This is a serious word to interject when arguing, and it should never be used, at any time in a marriage, as a threatening weapon against another. When in anger, a spouse carelessly and loosely injects this word into battle. The equally angry partner may impulsively up the ante and agree that divorce should be on the table, front and center. I have had divorced people tell me that they never intended for a divorce to happen, but throughout an argument, divorce was carelessly threatened. That rhetoric got out of hand and took on a life of its own. Due to pride and stubbornness, an argument progressed beyond what either spouse could have imagined or truly wanted. Backtracking and an apology should have stepped in and taken place, but pride and stubbornness kept the floor, and they would not allow recourse to happen. The result was divorce.

15. Don't Be Judgmental

Resist the temptation to see yourself as the standard your spouse must adhere to. Any standard for judgment must be in line with a proper understanding of God's Word and not your prejudices, preferences, or convictions. And please do not use Bible verses out of context or as a hammer.

There is a difference between making judgments, which both the Bible and life call upon us to do, and being judgmental. To be judgmental is to look down upon another in a condescending or holier-than-thou way and not to have all the facts (See John 7:24).

16. Apologize When You're Wrong

Humility goes a long way in ending arguments and removing animosity in both spouses. Owning one's wrongs is a key step in becoming right in your attitude and conduct. After owning it, confess it to your spouse. And remember, "Pride goeth before destruction, and an haughty spirit before a fall" (Proverbs 16:18 KJV).

17. Don't Fight in Front of Your Children

Children can be very fragile, even though they also can be very resilient. Children who witness fighting between parents can become fearful that the parents will hurt each other or get a divorce. Children often assume the blame for any fighting that takes place between their parents.

18. Fight in Front of Your Children

This appears contradictory to the prior point, but the difference is in *how* you fight. Some children have never seen their parents fighting, so they are disadvantaged in knowing how to fight fair when they marry. When you engage in fair fights as a married couple, you can be a powerful model for your children. That example will go a long way in helping your children learn the proper way to fight. This does not suggest that you should do all your fighting in front of your children. When children happen to be present, spouses must be aware that they should correct and clean up damaging forms of arguing and not leave a negative impact on their children's minds, while demonstrating the right way to fight, as suggested in the guidelines you are now reading.

19. Be Considerate

What is the backstory to the argument? What preceded the argument? Did your spouse have a hard day leading to a bad mood? Is there a bigger picture you are missing, such as your spouse retaliating against you over something? At times, it would be wise to table the matter as soon as possible and put a looming battle to rest before it escalates if you or your spouse is in a foul or less-than-desirous mood to discuss things.

20. Don't Walk Away

Doing so arbitrarily can frustrate and irritate your spouse. There can be good reasons to walk away, such as curtailing an argument that continues to escalate or putting an end to an endless discussion. But abruptly walking away without giving notice or expressing a legitimate reason disrupts the resolution process. And remember that what goes around, comes around. The tactics you use on your spouse may eventually come full circle as your spouse does the same thing to you in walking away.

21. Don't Play the Victim

It can be tempting to deflect the spotlight from your wrongs by eliciting pity. Phrases like, "OK, I'm the bad guy. I'm this horrible human being who causes all the trouble," "Pile it on. I deserve it," "I'm always to blame," or "I never do anything right," often causes one spouse to back off an issue being discussed in an attempt to reassure the "victim" spouse that no one is trying to imply that the victim spouse is a terrible person. Playing the victim card deflects attention from the issue being addressed, and a matter gets dropped—unresolved. Short and simple, it is marital blackmail. And this tactic will soon wear out its welcome with its hearer.

22. How You End the Argument Is Important

Ideally, ending an argument or discussion with a hug or kiss is nice. However, reality tells us this may be impractical for two people with momentary elevated blood pressures. The next best thing would be to come back soon and give hugs or kisses, along with the assuring words, "I love you." Then perhaps you might pray together. Prayer would be a great first step before arguing, but arguments are often spontaneous, and heads that are hot do not lend themselves to prayer at that time.

At intersections, you can take a right turn at a red stoplight, but you must first stop and make sure it's clear and safe before you go. You should not drift through the turn. When getting into an argument with your spouse, don't drift into deeper waters, but make a mental stop, assess where you are mentally and emotionally, and reflect on the rules for fair fighting. If you feel that you are getting into it before you even realize it, you are in serious need of reading and rereading the rules for fighting fair, almost to the point where recalling them becomes second nature. You can even go so far as posting them in the location where most of your fights occur, so your eyes remind your brain, which in turn, will remind your tongue.

When you are at an intersection governed by stop signs, stoplights, or roundabouts, you must yield to the motorist who has the right-of-way. In marriage, the right-of-way is acknowledging the right way to navigate marriage matters. Care, concern, and caution will add many miles to your marriage.

As you look into the mirror of marriage, what is reflected back to you when considering everyday interactions in your marriage? How do you handle the shortcomings of your spouse that clash with you and are ever before you? How would being honest in accurately seeing yourself allow you to better handle a spouse's foibles? Now, apply and implement the lessons you've learned as a part of your plan to better yourself, and trust that your actions as a good role-model will be a positive influence on your spouse.

CHAPTER 6

Trouble Brewing

WHEN SERIOUS STORMS IN NATURE form, funnel clouds may be taking shape, or ominous clouds gather overhead, or perhaps a threatening wind builds in intensity. One would think such obvious signs would garner serious attention from the observer. The wise would heed the obvious. It is no different in marriage. Prudent mates don't neglect early signs that warn of pending trouble with spouses. But those who ignore early warnings will ultimately find themselves unprepared to handle the level of damage that will be uncovered from such neglect in one's marriage.

What is your God-given calling as a mate? Is it not to love your partner in a way that tells him or her that you are paying attention to, showing caring concern for, and treating that personally chosen spouse as a treasured find? Where is your marriage heading? Or is it already there?

The apostle Paul addressed stress in marriage and built a case, showing the importance and value of being forewarned. This will allow us to be forearmed against what can counter marital success, which otherwise could eventually overcome a marriage.

> In view of the present distress … if you marry, you have not sinned …Yet such will have trouble in this life, and I am trying to spare you. (1 Corinthians 7:26, 28)

46

The above verse reflects Paul's concern about the many troubles in store for married couples. What is the "present distress" to which Paul alluded in verse 26? In his blog, Shawn Brasseaux[13] offers three explanations for the stress Paul spoke of. The first concerns the persecution that the Corinthian believers—and all believers of that day—might have faced for their faith. It was dangerous to be a Christian in the Roman Empire during the days of the apostle Paul. If the Christian were to marry and had to experience persecution or even martyrdom, concern by his or her spouse would only exacerbate feelings of worry or fear.

A second view centers on the carnality of the Corinthian church. The citizens of Corinth were known for their sensuality. Their city was home to the Temple of Aphrodite, where one thousand prostitutes were made available to its cultists.[14] Fleshly practices were performed as religious acts to pagan gods. That mindset of carnality most likely spilled over into the Corinthian church as individual citizens came to faith in Christ and joined the Corinthian congregation. They brought lifestyles and mindsets that needed to be purged of fleshly habits. Self-centered, fleshly minded individuals did not make good spouses. The place the church was at spiritually concerned Paul. He may have thought any such marriage-minded individual should wait until he or she achieved an evident level of spiritual maturity before marrying.

A third view is that marriage itself can bring trouble because of our human, fallen natures and the struggle we face against giving up self, as needed in marriage. If single, widowed, or divorced, Paul's advice was not to seek a mate. By staying single, an individual was more unencumbered and able to serve the Lord, even as Paul was and did.

---

[13] Shawn Brasseaux, "What Is the 'Present Distress' of 1 Corinthians 7:26?" *For What Saith the Scriptures,* Arc Ministries, November 24, 2018, https://forwhatsaiththescriptures.org/2018/11/24/present-distress-1-corinthians-7-26/.
[14] Charles F. Pfeiffer and Everett F. Harrison, *The Wycliffe Bible Commentary* (Chicago: Moody Press, 1962), 1,227.

Marriage lessons can be extrapolated from all three views. But despite Paul's concern for the difficult things that marriage could bring to individuals, he stated that if one chose to biblically proceed in marriage per God's blessing, one didn't sin by that action or desire.

> One who is married is concerned about the things of the world, how he may please his wife … one who is married is concerned about the things of the world, how she may please her husband. (1 Corinthians 7:33, 34)

The Innate Issues in Marriage

Troubles in marriage can come from many sources, from money struggles to in-law interference, but it mainly comes from within the participants themselves. Troubles often are exacerbated by outside sources, but they are not the root cause. Jesus said, "There is nothing outside the man which can defile him if it goes into him, but the things which proceed out of the man are what defile the man" (Mark 7:15).

If you are looking for trouble, you can find a lot of potential for it in marriage. I think it is safe to say that no individual enters marriage looking for trouble. But quite the opposite is true; couples enter marriage expecting marital enjoyment and success. However, Paul's admonition concerning marriage and troubles was not his assessment, but he spoke what the Holy Spirit had given him from God. God spoke these words to us through His servant Paul. And the root cause of marriage troubles is not the institution itself but the fallen nature of those who engage in it their way.

In this scripture passage, pleasing one's mate was coupled with legitimate concerns about the things of the world, indicating that a mate's attention would be divided—and necessarily so—for meeting life's responsibilities. When marriage happens, as in all of life, bills need to be paid, for couples cannot live on love, although some may think so. Meeting obligations and responsibilities, both inside and outside the home, requires significant time commitments, which can leave couples emotionally and physically drained and with little left in the tank to enjoy quiet moments with each other. You add children to the mix, and you may be fortunate to find any time to be together for R&R.

Newlyweds can and should enjoy many days of wedded bliss, but eventually as life moves on, schedules get busy. Additionally, this new experience of marriage can lose its luster. Over time, mates who have been coupled together may find that the bloom had faded from the rose. This assessment is not to discourage young couples but to prepare them for two realities in marriage. First, as things continue to get busy in their lives, they will not have an abundance of time together. Second, constant attention to maintaining love will be required to make a marriage solid and successful, but other life obligations will vie for a spouse's attention.

Giving needed attention to the responsibilities of life can siphon off available time, leaving little time for marital interests. Earning an income, accumulating needed or wanted possessions while also maintaining what you already own, trying to develop a nest egg, having and rearing children, and being involved in one's church and community take a toll on a couple's available time. If a couple is not careful about consistently nurturing their marriage relationship, over time, a husband and wife may find themselves strangers to each other and light years apart. This is especially true when children are added to the picture because parents invest much time in their children. Eventually, those children leave home, and Dad and Mom are left in their wake. Will this couple survive the new reality in their relationship?

Unfortunately, couples too often do not sense or choose to ignore the myriad of storms and chill winds that take place throughout the years of marriage. Their relationship pays a price that shows up in their later years.

Preparing for Storms

When a couple wakes up later in life and sees the destruction that the storms have done to their marriage, the spouses are stunned. You ask, "What storms?" They are storms of unresolved, pent-up volatility from years of marital neglect and misunderstandings, which the couple never took the time to talk out and resolve, leaving a residue of hurt or resentment that accumulated and festered. The storm damage contributed to each spouse becoming embedded in separate lifestyles and routines. When they try to come together later – if even they desire to do so - those separate, established lifestyles and routines clash.

Be forewarned if you currently have children in your home. As much as children can be a joy and blessing, their presence can also overshadow a marriage if Dad and Mom do not practice due diligence in prioritizing being husband and wife. A thriving marriage is not about finding time for you and your spouse but *committing* to establishing time to keep your love relationship solid.

Think of it this way. You have a fishbowl. In that bowl, you place your family schedule. Knowing the bowl has limited space, you would be wise to first place within that bowl the most-important items: your family values, such as necessary time devoted to spiritual matters and developing and maintaining interpersonal relationships. Once the most important items are in the bowl, you can add other important, yet less significant items. These lesser items can fill in the pockets and cavities around the larger items. If you first fill the bowl with smaller and less important items, there is the danger of running out of adequate space for the needed, larger, and more-valued items, one of which is to nourish and maintain a healthy relationship with your spouse. This item should be among the priority items in the bowl, along with spiritual matters, but unfortunately, that often is not the case.

I have a dear friend whose wedding I conducted eons ago. Every so often, I run into him. He is quick to remind me of the best piece of marriage advice I gave him and his wife at their wedding: "Establish a weekly date night," I said. Despite all that was involved in him and his wife rearing three children, who had extensive extracurricular school calendars, and having a busy work schedule, which put two cell phones on the husband's hips (a phone for each business), he has told me that over the years they have jealously guarded and faithfully kept their weekly Friday night date time, even to this day. He credits that consistent date night as a contributing factor in keeping them together in a healthy relationship. From my perspective, they appear to remain happily married.

Some may push back on this point. Some might argue that the couple in the example above could keep their marriage fresh by going out on date nights because they had the money to do so, while also having the money to pay for a babysitter, but that is not a luxury every couple enjoys. Some couples may feel that they don't have the time, money, or energy to keep the marriage relationship a priority. Obviously, I don't know the particulars of my readers' circumstances or environments. All I can do is appeal to any married couple not to let the marriage fire be reduced to embers. Get a friend to babysit. Share an ice-cream cone with your spouse at McDonald's. Have something to look forward to weekly, even if it's cheap or short in duration. After the kids are in bed, sit down and share a piece of pie at the table. Do something that brings you together weekly (at the least). And by all means, keep the fires burning in the bedroom!

CHAPTER 7

The Excuses

FOR YEARS, I HAVE WATCHED and been a fan of the cable show *Little People, Big World*. I was surprised and saddened to see the relationship between the father and mother, Matt and Amy, end in divorce. Throughout the show's seasons, Matt would reference how different he and Amy were as their arguments and disagreements aired in front of a national T.V. audience. Then we learned of the divorce.

Afterward and on occasion, Matt would echo that the cause of the divorce was because he and Amy were so different. He saw himself as more aggressive and a go-getter in life, as opposed to Amy's conservative and reflective nature, which made her slower and more cautious in arriving at decisions. To Matt, those lifestyles butted heads. If I had had the opportunity to counsel them, I would have kindly challenged Matt with the truth that their divorce was not because they were too different but rather because one or both was not willing to change and adapt to the point of compromise and learn to walk together in the light of their wedding vows.

Being the Same or Different—Does It Matter?

Along with Matt, others join the we're-too-different refrain as the reason for divorce. I could put under two headings the list of reasons people had given me for justifying their needs or wants for divorces from their mates. Those headings would be "We're Too Different" or "We're Too Much Alike." Interesting, isn't it? On the one hand, we have people convinced that their marriage woes are based on being too different as a couple. They highlight their differences to underscore their point. Yet on the other hand, some believe that all their marital conflict is due to being too much alike. They, too, delineate all the ways being alike has caused problems. Which one is it? Is being too different as a couple the reason for marital discord and divorce, or is being too alike the cause of friction and separation?

Years ago, I performed the wedding ceremony of a young couple who was part of a church I was pastoring. They were like two peas in a pod. They were so much alike in so many ways. They had laid-back, easygoing personalities that would make one think they were a perfect match for each other. Some years later, the husband died. Two years after that, the wife remarried. This time she married a man who was her exact opposite in many ways. I lost contact with her. Over time, we bumped into each other, and I had the opportunity to ask, "Is it better to marry someone just like you or someone who is your opposite?"

Her answer was, "It doesn't matter. Each has its own problems."

When conducting premarital or marriage counseling, I inform my counselees that a successful marriage is not based on finding the right person but on becoming the right person. Do not misunderstand me. Seeking the right person is a noble goal, but it will assure nothing. However, I give you a caveat about choosing a mate in Appendix 4.

As much as you try and as committed as you might be to your marriage, there are no marriage assurances. You cannot control your spouse. You can only be the best version of yourself while committing yourself to rest in the Lord. I was recently told of a godly couple whom I have known for many years. After eighteen years of marriage and out of the blue, the formerly committed-to-the-Lord-and-His-ways husband informed his wife that he was no longer interested in Christianity or being married. He left his wife and family, only to take up residence with a coworker.

Again, there are no guarantees in marriage. The only control you have as a partner in a marriage is over yourself—or should have over yourself. But unfortunately, some people have yet to learn how to control themselves. When facing the many troubles in marriage, these people are in danger of falling apart and self-destructing when they most need to stand strong. You may think you married the right one, who is just like you, loves the Lord as you do, and enjoys many of the same things that you do, only to find later that your marriage has crumbled, perhaps through no fault of your own.

You have no control over your mate changing or not changing. However, you may have influence. Your wrong behavior may call your actions into question if a spouse has lost interest in continuing the marriage. But I must be quick to add that each individual is accountable for his or her own actions, so any blame cannot be automatically assumed and foisted on yourself or on another. Questionable actions and decisions by a distant or estranged spouse do not justify shifting blame or responsibility onto the remaining party, nor should one party feel exonerated because it was the other spouse who departed or is living estranged. Estrangement should require a lot of needed soul-searching—on both parts.

In addition to asking for God's help, the best that spouses can do is work on themselves and be all they can be, regardless of the things that life and uncaring spouses throw at them. If you try to control your mate's love for you by pushing and directing him or her to do so, it will not work. Your mate must love you out of his or her will and heart. You cannot convince or coerce a spouse into doing so against his or her will. Groveling or begging to be loved will not work.

I have found in my counseling ministry that when a desperate spouse begs or grovels to keep a departing mate, the one leaving often adopts the view that the desperate spouse is weak and needy, which underscores, in his or her mind, the decision to leave. This further alienates and empowers the disinterested mate to act in a cavalier manner regarding matters between the couple.

As for my wife and me, we dated for three years during college. After graduation, we prepared for marriage by going our separate ways for a year. She returned to her home in New England, and I returned to my roots in Pennsylvania, which were quite different backgrounds. She had grown up in a city suburb of Boston, and I had grown up in a small farming community in Pennsylvania.

During our time apart, we worked and saved money for the wedding while getting to know each other differently—through letters, extended time apart, and occasional visits. We needed to test our love and see if it was more than just a college romance. We felt that if our love was the real deal, it would survive the test of time and separation. It would help us determine whether absence made the heart grow fonder or prone to wonder and wander. After those four years of dating and talking, we felt confident that we were 97 percent compatible. We agreed on virtually everything, or so we thought.

But throughout our marriage, we have found that we are quite different in various ways. I somewhat chuckle when I hear unmarried couples say that they are living together before marriage to see if they are compatible. They tie the knot when everything seems to work out in the short haul. Too often, such couples divorce after claiming they found themselves too different from each other or too much alike.

I conclude living together before marriage is a shaky strategy for most, if not all. I cite a number of reasons. First, marriage will show you just how different you are as a couple over time, even though you may be alike in many ways or vice-versa. Second, you will change during your marriage and life, and your mate will too. God, in His wisdom, designed marriage as a lifelong commitment to counter and overcome the changing picture of life. Change can be destructive if one allows it. That's why marriage calls for us to stretch our love, which I will explain in a later chapter. We must become better individuals and partners than we were when we first married.

Third, various studies reflect the negative results of living together before marriage. In a lecture to some four thousand single adults, Pastor Tommy Nelson of the Denton Bible Church in Denton, Texas, spoke of a study that found 80 percent of those who live together before marriage will divorce, 60 percent of those married by a justice of the peace will divorce, and 40 percent of those married in churches will divorce. But out of those who read and study the Bible daily, only one out of every 1,051 people will divorce.[15] Those are sobering conclusions.

Potential brides, you will not determine Mr. Right by first living with him, for there is no Mr. Right. One day in the future you might find yourself saying, "I thought I married Mr. Right until I learned his first name was Always!" In the same way, a man will not discover Mrs. Right by first living with her. It is said that the one constant in life is *change*. It is built into your marriage (and in all of life), whether you like it or not. Quite often, the change will not be what you want or like, for there will be many things that you will have no control over, other than over yourself, if you put in the work.

Learning to Become Mr. or Mrs. Right

You don't marry as Mr. and Mrs. Right. Couples achieve a successful marriage by learning to *become* Mr. and Mrs. Right. For years, I was an optimist who always saw the bright side

---

[15] Tommy Nelson, "The Art of Intimacy, Part 1," *Family Life Today* podcast, February 2, 2007, https://www.familylife.com/podcast/familylife-today/the-art-of-intimacy-part-1/.

of things. It was a characteristic that my wife was attracted to and appreciated, especially because early on, she acknowledged herself as more of a pessimist (She now classifies herself as a realist more than a pessimist, and I concur, but she still likes those Hallmark shows). Over time, I have changed and become more of a pragmatist or realist. Marriage and life can do that to you.

For instance, we recently bought another car. My wife wanted to keep our older car to be used as a backup car. We also own a pickup truck. In the past, because of my so-called easygoing (avoider?) nature, which had allowed my positive mindset, I would have nodded my agreement to her wish, but now I had changed. At this point in my life (and age), I became more of a pragmatist, and I did not want the added headache of another car's upkeep (oil changes, tires, and other maintenance), insurance, and my state's annual car tax. Besides that, keeping the third vehicle also took up driveway space, which would be a problem when weekly family gatherings brought anywhere from nine-to-eleven cars, which vied for parking spaces. None of those things would have fazed me in the past, but times and things had changed, and I had too.

But out of the love and respect for my wife, which has been nurtured and grown over the years, I agreed to retain the extra car as a backup. On the flip side, I am convinced that if a strong desire to downsize had remained my focus and that I had chosen to lighten my responsibility load by having one less car to take care of, my wife would have respectfully and lovingly concurred.

It has been said that a man goes into marriage hoping the woman will never change because during courting, he is used to being treated so well—even doted upon—and a woman goes into marriage hoping to change the man, for she sees a lot that needs changed. Like it or not, we all change throughout life. Change, along with death and taxes, is another certainty in life you can count on.

Perhaps as a mate, you are discouraged over things that have changed or not changed in your marriage. As a wife, you may have hoped that the love you lavished on your husband would certainly have positively changed him throughout your marriage as he saw how devoted, sacrificial, and caring you were of him. After all, any change you encouraged in or for him would have been for his good. You may have reasoned in marriage that you could change the things you saw in him while dating, which you did not care for, by your loving words and actions as his wife. But through it all, he has not changed. Perhaps he *has* changed from the good you first saw in him to what he now shows himself to actually be—not terribly loving or caring.

Conversely, as a husband, you have worked hard and diligently in doing your part to contribute to your family's needs and security. However, to your wife, what you do in contributing seems to never be enough. She rarely seems satisfied with you or the things you have done or not done. You were happy with your relationship before marriage. Once you married her, she changed, or so you think. Now you feel you have a mother instead of a wife. During the dating and engagement days, she accepted you as you were, but now you find that is not the case. Perhaps you see her as nagging, pushing, demanding, and dissatisfied with you. This has left you frustrated, unhappy, and feeling misled.

As a husband or wife, if you are talking about divorce or are unhappy in your marriage, please consider your root problem may have little to do with the person you married, who is so different from you or too alike. Rather, it may be because one or both of you in the marriage will not work to identify and overcome the individual problems that each of you brought into the marriage. *Unfortunately, positive effort exerted by one mate alone may prove inadequate to carry an unbalanced marriage to success.*

As you continue looking into the mirror of marriage, can you identify any excuses you have embraced to justify wrong behavior on your part? What problems arise that lead you to think your marriage problems stem from being too much like or too different from your spouse? Take away the too alike or too different equation and see if you can write down any reasons or excuses you have told yourself or others about why your marriage is not working or cannot work.

CHAPTER 8

Marriage—Happy or Holy?

GOD'S ULTIMATE DESIGN FOR MARRIAGE is not to make us happy but to make us holy. That sentence may be stunning to some. One might think that God wants us to be happy in marriage; otherwise, why get married? *Get married to be miserable? No thanks.* Yet how many marriages operate in misery rather than functioning as God intended them to be?

Do not misunderstand the opening paragraph, for God certainly desires every God-ordained marriage to be happy (As an aside, some people conveniently use God-ordained marriage as a scapegoat for leaving a marriage, rationalizing that their bad marriage must be due to it not having been God-ordained). But we must realize that happiness comes through holiness. The more each marriage partner conforms to the image of Christ, the more that individual will display Christlike attitudes. The more Christlike the attitudes displayed by both in a marriage, the better the odds are for becoming a happier and fulfilled couple.

Changing to a Christlike Spouse

In my marriage, I was the spouse who was influenced to change when my wife initially took it upon herself to change. She focused more on conforming to the image of Christ and therefore, became more like Him than ever before. Where did she start? She memorized Philippians 2:5-11.

> Have this attitude in yourselves which was also in Christ Jesus, who, although He existed in the form of God, did not regard equality with God a thing to be grasped, but emptied Himself, taking the form of a bond-servant, *and* being made in the likeness of men. Being found in appearance as a man, He humbled Himself by becoming obedient to the point of death, even death on a cross. For this reason also, God highly exalted Him, and bestowed on Him the name which is above every name, so that at the name of Jesus EVERY KNEE WILL BOW, of those who are in heaven and on earth and under the earth, and that every tongue will confess that Jesus Christ is Lord, to the glory of God the Father.

My wife adopted a lifestyle and mindset of pursuing humility and servanthood as she endeavored to live out her commitment, both to her Lord and to her marriage, and it became another part of the impetus for my change. However, there is no guarantee that the same thing will happen for you, but regardless, you will become a better person for your efforts in committing to the mindset of Christ. But a word of balance is needed. To have the mindset of Christ does not mean turning yourself into a doormat for others to walk on.

Outside of the Lord's direct intervention, the best opportunity that a mate will have to change a partner will be to first change himself or herself, by purging selfish habits, damaging actions, and inflammatory speech, which come between one mate and another. We could label this as God's indirect intervention. This means that change came from God indirectly and through individuals who applied God's truths to their personal lives and then to their marriages.

Consider that every aspect of a Christian's life should be about becoming holy. To have the mind of Christ is to strive to be pleasing to God in all ways. The word *holy* means *separation to God,*[16] even as God is separate and distinct from the fallen nature of humankind. God is separated from sin. His holiness is always the whole standard of moral excellence. In this vein, we could define God's holiness as His being wholly, as in wholly complete. This character of holiness is God's desire to be in all of those who choose to submit wholly to Him and live a life of honor before Him.

Be holy, for I am holy. (1 Peter 1:16 NKJV)

Failing marriages are like tires going flat. It's rarely a blowout but usually a slow leak. Doing your part in seeking to prevent your marriage from slowly deflating over time will require you to refuse to remain as you are if you know damaging things about yourself within the marriage. God clearly set the destination every Christian is to strive for: to become more like the character of God's Son. You may be familiar with the lesson we can apply from the marriage triangle.

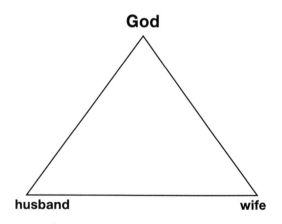

The destination for both the Christian husband and wife is clear. Meeting at the top is the best way to be brought together. The

---

[16] "G38—*Hagiasmos,*" *Strong's Greek Lexicon (KJV)*, Blue Letter Bible, https://www.blueletterbible.org/lexicon/g38/kjv/tr/0-1/.

more each spouse continues ascending in his or her relationship with God, the closer they draw together as a couple. How tied together did God make the first husband and wife? It was so close that one actually was created out of the other. How tight are couples made through marriage? They are made so tight by God they are to become what He declares them to be - *one*.

> The Lord God fashioned into a woman the rib which He had taken from the man, and brought her to the man. The man said, "This is bone of my bones; And flesh of my flesh." (Genesis 2:22–23).

The Bible expositor Matthew Henry said, "The woman was made of a rib out of the side of Adam; not made out of his head to rule over him, nor out of his feet to be trampled upon by him, but out of his side to be equal with him, under his arm to be protected, and near his heart to be beloved." [17] When a husband finds excellence in the woman he marries, he should consider himself extremely blessed, and he should let his wife know it.

> An excellent wife, who can find? For her worth is far above jewels. The heart of her husband trusts in her, and he will have no lack of gain. She does him good and not evil all the days of her life. (Proverbs 31:10–12 NASB)

Unfortunately, sin separates, and due to humanity's rebellion against God, the fallen nature within each of us can and has wreaked havoc on relationships. We must battle against letting that happen in our sphere of influence.

---

[17] Matthew Henry and Samuel Palmer. *An Exposition of the Old and New Testament,* Volume 6 (United States: Haswell, Barrington, and Haswell, 1838), 36.

If your mate's heart is hardened, you must look into the mirror of marriage and ask yourself if you possibly had a role in that happening. Did your wrong conduct allow your heart to harden? In saying this, I reiterate what I said earlier in the book: I am not attempting to blame the victim, who may be an innocent party, for I am not suggesting that your spouse has the right to shift blame onto you for his or her wrong actions.

Each individual is personally accountable for his or her own actions. Yet I also know that no spouse in a marriage is perfectly innocent in marital relationships. Since we know that no one is perfect, I am not addressing the need for perfection in your life as a marriage partner, but rather, I'm touching on what reasonable conduct and interaction should be shown to your spouse. Your mate may be the one with the hardened heart, whose wrongful spirit can in no way honestly fall on you. Regardless of where you find yourself in your marriage relationship, your way out and up in life and your spirit will be through holiness or godliness, whether your mate does or does not join you in the process or you think you may have had any part in your spouse's pulling away or disinterest.

What Does a Wife Want in Her Marriage?

Husbands, love your wives, just as Christ also loved the church and gave Himself up for her. So husbands ought also ought to love their own wives as their own bodies. He who loves his own wife loves himself; for no one ever hated his own flesh, but nourishes and cherishes it, just as Christ also *does* the church, because we are parts of His body. FOR THIS REASON A MAN SHALL LEAVE HIS FATHER AND HIS MOTHER AND BE JOINED TO HIS WIFE, AND THE TWO SHALL BECOME ONE FLESH. (Ephesians 5:25, 28-31)

During my counseling years, many wives expressed a yearning for a deep spiritual connection of oneness with their husbands. Generally speaking, Christian women desire their husbands to pray with them, interact in the scriptures with them, and lead their homes and marriages in spiritual matters. These desires significantly outpace other wishes that Christian wives have expressed to me.

But here is a cause for women to pause. In counseling sessions with husbands and in the presence of their wives, various husbands reported that when they attempted to spiritually lead their homes, some wives denigrated their leadership attempts as lacking and never good enough. Some husbands got discouraged and gave up.

Wives, reflect on whether you are a help or hindrance in your husband's stepping up to his leadership role. Do you say the right thing the wrong way? Are you idealistic in your expectations of your husband's spiritual leadership skills? Do you give him little latitude in learning how to grow into the role? What can you do to help him take the lead? Do you have kind words that would encourage his desire to step up or stay in his endeavor to lead? Does any nonverbal communication emanate from you that may give bad vibes to your husband in this area?

What Does a Husband Want?

> Her husband is respected at the city gate, where he takes his seat among the elders of the land. (Proverbs 31:23 NIV)

Plain and simple, respect is a husband's major desire (women and wives also want to be respected). Most husbands I have heard from want wives who recognize and acknowledge their efforts to improve their families' welfare. I use Gary Chapman's *The 5 Love Languages* as part of my counseling repertoire. These five languages are receiving gifts, physical touch, acts of service, quality time, and words of affirmation. For those unfamiliar with these five points, Dr. Chapman identifies these points to determine how one can love a spouse in the way the spouse wants to be loved.[18]

As a mate, you may think you are showing your spouse love when you give him or her a gift. To you, gift-giving is showing love because you love to receive gifts. Receiving gifts is your language, but for your spouse, receiving a gift from you may say little to him or her. If your mate's love language is acts of service, your mate will feel more loved by you if you help with projects around the house. Speak love to your spouse by giving the gift that identifies most with what he or she likes.

In counseling, I have overwhelmingly found that most men desire the love language of hearing words of affirmation. I have identified it as my love language. Yet I told my wife that I do not need or want to hear a daily dose or weekly stream of appreciative words. Hearing appreciation from her here and there throughout the year is all I need. What would get the wrong kind of attention from me would be once-in-a-decade words of appreciation from my wife. Then I would feel my efforts were unnoticed, under-noticed, or unappreciated, and I would be tempted to not continue to put forth any extra work effort for her.

Being a godly wife or husband takes a lot of work—on oneself. When concerted effort is not put forth by either or both partners, a spouse might find oneself in a lonely world. As surprising as it may seem, loneliness often becomes a major problem in marriage. You may ask, "How can that be?" Here is a couple who live, eat, sleep, raise children, and vacation together, yet one or both are lonely? You may either be thinking, *I don't get it,* or *I completely understand.*

---

[18] Gary D. Chapman, *The Five Love Languages: The Secret to Love that Lasts* (Chicago: Moody Publishers, 2015).

You may not have felt loneliness in your marriage, but you could be headed there unless you work to change and make yourself pleasing to live with. Even then, your spouse may not be willing to put in the necessary work to fend off the loneliness in you or in him or her. If you are a Christian, you have the added advantage of God's help in curtailing any damaging behavior you might bring to the marriage, while you learn how to deal with the destructive behavior of a spouse who may have little desire to correct his or her wrongs. Your spouse may be content with the status quo, whereas you are not. Left to ourselves in our sinfulness, the Bible informs us that we turn inward to our own desires and wishes.

> All we like sheep have gone astray; We have turned,
> every one, to his own way. (Isaiah 53:6 NKJV)

When gazing into that mirror of marriage, it is important for any married individual to see and recognize his or her penchant for that inward bent. To counter, once having one's own mind set properly, it will allow us to be other-minded if we want to have marital success, which is not only true in married life but also in all of life's relationships—especially those in the body of Christ. Christians must not only learn how to get along but also to love one another as Christ has loved us.

Continuing your look into the mirror of marriage, do you reflect more of a commitment to being happy or holy in marriage? What is your priority? What do you believe your mate's priority is? If your priority is holiness first, the next chapter is for you.

CHAPTER 9

Growing in Holiness

IF ONE SEEKS TO EXPERIENCE marriage as God intended it to be, it will require growth and positive change. When a person surrenders their heart to the Lord and accepts His forgiveness, God declares that person immediately sanctified or set apart to God. The New Testament refers to this as God declaring and naming Christians as saints. In this declared position, Christians are then instructed as saints to walk out this declaration of holiness with a matching lifestyle of purity in an everyday mindset of priorities, decisions, deeds, and responses to life and all it entails.

> We have been sanctified [set apart to God][19] through
> the offering of the body of Jesus Christ once for all.
> (Hebrews 10:10)
> Be ye holy; for I am holy. (1 Peter 1:16 KJV, our
> living responsibility to God)

How do we grow in a holiness that produces positive change in our lives and brings joy to our relationships and glory to God? Many of Christ's teachings were given in an outdoor, agricultural environment. Growing up in a farming community, I learned

---

[19] "G38—Hagiasmos," *Strong's Greek Lexicon* (*KJV*), Blue Letter Bible, https://www.blueletterbible.org/lexicon/g38/kjv/tr/0-1/.

to appreciate the process that brings things to harvest. Using the agricultural model to explain how to grow in holiness, I will begin where both Christ and farmers start: with the soil (See Mark 4:4–8).

Till the Soil

Cold weather can result in frozen ground, which eventually thaws in spring, but after the thawing process, the ground remains somewhat stiff, as it has a thin layer of crust on it. Even when ground that never freezes because of a warmer climate is left unused, it is subject to pounding rain, which leaves the soil compacted to where it needs to have its soil plowed or cultivated. This is a necessary step in preparing soil to receive seeds. The process of tilling or breaking up the soil allows the seed to settle into the heart of the four-to-six-inch-deep, nutrient-filled topsoil, where all the sprouting action of the seed happens.

In the parable of the four soils, found in Mark 4, I believe the soils represent the spiritual heart. Here are but a few examples of what the Bible reveals about the heart:

- Above all else, guard your heart, for everything you do flows from it. (Proverbs 4:23 NIV)
- Blessed are the pure in heart. (Matthew 5:8)
- Create in me a clean heart, O God, and renew a right spirit within me. (Psalm 51:10 KJV)
- You shall love the Lord your God with all your heart, and with all your soul, and with all your strength, and with all your mind; and your neighbor as yourself. (Luke 10:27)

A believer is responsible for preparing and guarding his or her heart so that it does not become hard, lazy, or unattended—no crust forms over it due to inactivity, inattention, or hardness. Aeration of the soil is necessary for germination. Simply put, a seed cannot do its work if the soil is not loose. Keeping the soil (heart) pliable requires one to remain intentional. It is accomplished spiritually through a willing spirit, Bible input, prayer, confession of sin that restores fellowship with God, and application of truths as God reveals or reminds one of them. In all of life (particularly marriage), the heart must remain soft and pliable so that God and holiness can do their intended work in and through one's everyday life. The Bible warns against a heart of stone (See Ezekiel 11:19 and 36:26).

Plant Seed

The seed represents the Word of God. We can get God's Word into our lives in five ways: hearing, reading, studying, memorizing, and meditating on it. I propose a little exercise for you. Let your pinkie finger represent *hearing* God's Word. Try to grip a copy of the Bible and pick it up with only that finger. Yes, I agree; it was silly even to try or suggest. The Bible states, "Faith comes by hearing, and hearing by the word of God" (Romans 10:17 NKJV), so hearing God's Word appears to be very important. Yet we are warned that only hearing God's Word will not suffice, for James tells us to be "doers of the word, and not hearers only, deceiving yourselves" (James 1:22 NKJV).

Moving on, use your pinkie and ring finger together and try to grip the Bible and lift it. The pinkie is *hearing* God's Word, and the ring finger represents *reading* God's Word. In using these two fingers, the grip somewhat improves, but it's tenuous at best.

Use your pinkie, ring finger, and center finger to grip the Bible and pick it up. Don't rest the Bible against your palm while using those three fingers. Use only your fingers. The center finger represents *studying* God's Word.

Now try gripping the Bible with your pinkie, ring, center, and index fingers. The index finger represents *memorizing* God's Word. Different configurations in using those four digits may allow for a better grip, but it is not even close to what you will need to firmly grasp either a physical Bible or God's Word.

Thus far, you have used four fingers that represent hearing, reading, studying, and memorizing God's Word. Now add your thumb to the mix. See what kind of a grip you can get while picking up and holding the Bible with all five fingers—case closed. The thumb represents *meditating* on God's Word. Meditation is done by applying the Word, after chewing on it in your mind and digesting its ideas. It is the process of thinking through, giving shape to, and doing something with what God reveals from hearing, reading, studying, or memorizing the Word.

From my experience, I would guess that the average church attender is mostly a hearer of God's Word, if he or she is actually listening. Preachers joke that if you ever want to see the dead come back to life, end the sermon. Some might even take the extra step of reading the Bible, but I have found that few Christians, comparatively speaking, employ each of the remaining three digits on the hand. Few Christians study the Bible, fewer still memorize any portions of the Bible, and even fewer meditate for life application on truths from the Bible.

To plant God's seed into your life will require you to be a person of the Word, meaning you incorporate biblical truths into your thinking and actions. Listening to the Bible through sermons or by other means, reading the Bible for yourself, studying the Bible, memorizing Bible verses that address salient points in your life, and then meditating on how to apply what you've learned are the key ways to plant God's Word or seed into your life. Also, join a Bible study group or enroll in programs that promote specific Bible interests that you have.

Water the Seed

Watering a field is a farmer's means of keeping the soil soft while also swelling and loosening the shell of the planted seed, which then allows the seed to crack open. Water provides the means for the germination process to begin inside the seed—a miraculous design by a creative God.

When we apply the idea of watering the seed spiritually, we understand that water is there to spur spiritual growth. The water of the Word is there to crack us open or open up our hearts so that we can be receptive to God's will for our lives and marriages. As you engage in the spiritual disciplines that God's Word calls for, spiritual germination occurs. Water brings refreshment and revitalizes, so the things in the Christian walk that align with God's calling qualify as watering your seed. Hearing, reading, studying, memorizing, and meditating on God's Word, prayer, fellowship, witnessing, Christian service, etc., are but a few of the many ways you can refresh the spiritual seed within your heart. The refreshing water of the living and written Word can restore and replenish the worst parched and wilted hearts.

Weed the Field and Garden

Any farmer or gardener has a deep disdain for weeds. Constant vigilance against them is needed because they grow so easily and quickly, with no need of a gardener—they seemingly spring up overnight. They present an immediate threat in competition with the seed for the nutrients and water in the soil. In your marriage, you must always be alert to those seemingly innocuous "weeds" that can crop up every day, such as a carelessly spoken word that could be taken the wrong way or momentary flashes of a cavalier spirit toward a spouse. If left unattended and allowed to accumulate, such unguarded actions or words can thwart the growth of the seed within the hearts of both spouses.

What are some other serious weeds that can threaten a marriage? Another weed is allowing unhealthy distance to grow between you and your mate by turning to or prioritizing other things or people. If you permit resentment to build and remain between you and your spouse, allow the slow erosion and eventual loss of physical affection, and hold onto offenses from words that wound, these negative things eventually overwhelm your marriage.

If allowed to, numerous strains of weeds in fields and gardens grow wild and out of control. If you ignore tending the garden or fields of your life, other things will vie for your time and attention and grow wild and possibly out of control. The Christian experience is not always a battle between good and evil and right or wrong. Sometimes the battle is between good, better, and best. Ask yourself what it will take to have a good marriage, an even better marriage, or the best marriage you could have. Work and weed toward the best you can have.

In a former ministry of mine, there was a family who, for years, faithfully attended worship services and was involved in the everyday life of the church. I would say that the parents appeared to have a good marriage. Their youngest son was a promising athlete, and they moved to a part of the country that was a hotbed for the sport that their son excelled in. For several years, the regimen required to excel in that sport continued to increase—so much so that other family routines had to fall in line behind the priority focus, which was increasing the young son's ability to secure a professional sports contract.

Spiritual matters gradually fell by the way, and eventually, the professional dream did not pan out as they had hoped it would. Unfortunately, not only did the sports dream die but also the relationships of those involved were negatively affected and strained. The fallout from the growth of the unchecked weeds took its toll, and the damage remains to this day. Church attendance and involvement have become a thing of the past for this family. In the wake left behind I have witnessed broken lives, and relationship estrangements, and battling of addictions. I sadly continue to witness the demise from afar, of a family I enjoyed being around, and I continue to pray for.

Feed the Soil

Adding fertilizer enriches the soil and replaces nutrients that the plants use up. As an aside for reading enjoyment, in farmer's terminology, certain fertilizer in liquid form is referred to as country perfume. Drive past a farmer's fields during certain times of the year, and you'll be "privileged" to inhale this special mixture. To give you a hint: it doesn't smell good.

To enrich the soil of your heart and make you more amenable to marriage as it ought to be, make it a practice together to attend marriage seminars, Bible study groups, Sunday school classes, worship services, and other similar things that will add strength to your spiritual and physical relationship with your mate. Get involved in a service ministry at your church. Taking in spiritual things will not be enough. You also must give out as spiritual input directs you to. Feeding spiritual soil is much like breathing. Anything living must breathe, which is a continual process of the in-and-out motion of the lungs. To constantly take in and not give out will make one stagnant. Constantly giving out without taking in will eventually suffocate you, physically and emotionally. Nutrients added to the soil must be done in a balanced way. Spiritual growth also requires the balance of taking in and giving out.

Protect Growth

Farmers use sprays, retardants, and pesticides. A backyard gardener might employ scarecrows, screening, netting, fences, and garden-variety sprays to keep out animals and destructive bugs.

What things are destructive to a marriage or spiritual growth? Let's go back to the four soils that Christ mentioned in Mark 4. Christ notes things that destroyed the growth of the seed: the troubles of life, the deceitfulness of pursuing riches, and worrying about the same things the world worries about (keeping up with the Joneses, accumulating bigger and better things, fame, power, prestige, etc.).

These things choke the seed and bring spiritual things to naught. The desires for other things may not be wrong in and of themselves, but they may follow the principle that sometimes good things become the enemy of better or best things. The text in Mark 4 notes that some individuals start out joyfully receiving the seed or hearing the Word, only to fizzle out somewhere down the road.

What does protecting a harvest look like? It is protecting the heart, the mind, biblical priorities, the schedule, correct commitments, the family, and marriage. Make yourself accountable to someone (If you are married, be accountable to your mate). Stay involved in the church.

Not forsaking our own assembling together, as is the habit of some. (Hebrews 10:25)

When you allow yourself or your marriage to withdraw from the church, you are on a slippery slope away from seeing growth and change in your life and marriage. You risk greatly diminishing your chances of experiencing marriage as God intended it to be.

But some may ask, what about people who don't go to church and non-Christian marriages? Can these marriages succeed? Yes, they can. Any marriage can be a success if it incorporates biblical principles into it. I believe many secular marriages do so, without even realizing it. But Christians have the advantage and unique ability as followers of Christ, to realize and attain marriage as God intended it to be, in all its fullness.

Rely on the Sun/Son

You can plant, water, weed, fertilize, and protect your seed all you want, physically, and still receive no harvest—if nature's *sun* doesn't cooperate. The sun or some light source is mandatory for crop development. We must coordinate all our human efforts with these critical elements to harvest a successful crop. Any successful spiritual harvest will require God's *Son* to be front and center in our lives and efforts. The words of Jesus make things crystal clear to us regarding the part Christ plays in all the efforts and results of Christians.

Apart from Me you can do nothing. (John 15:5)

Seeing ourselves clearly in the mirror of marriage will show how much a happy, successful, and lasting marriage depends on Him and our cooperation with Him. Marriage will reveal problem areas and shortcomings within us; however, we may not see those revelations without a concerted and intentional effort to examine ourselves as we really are. The Bible helps us to do that. The Son's part involves changing us from what we are to what we ought to be. Our part is to allow Him access to our wills and hearts to do so. Growing in holiness allows transformation to happen.

As you again look into the mirror of marriage, where do you come up short in your farming chores? Is your soil unprepared? Have you not been planting? Have you failed to weed as you should? What about protecting your crop? Identify your areas of shortcomings, evaluate the whys of each case, and fashion a plan for positive change.

CHAPTER 10

Stretching One's Love

AS ONE AGES, THE CONSCIOUS need for physical stretching becomes more pronounced, for the aging body's natural resilience to springing back into shape becomes a thing of the past. But despite knowing the benefits, the worn body doesn't want to go to that needed place called exercise. Comic relief tells us that God helps elderly folks battle this dilemma by designing senior citizens to become less coordinated, resulting in them constantly dropping things. This tendency to drop things necessitates them to bend repeatedly to pick up those many dropped items. The need to exercise and stretch aging bodies – solved.

Returning to a more serious note, resilience in life is necessary for more than just physical health. Consider the words of the apostle Peter: "Above all things have fervent love one for another, for 'love will cover a multitude of sins'" (1 Peter 4:8 NKJV). The context of this verse speaks about love among the body of Christian believers—those you worship with and are in relationship as a community. But realize, other Scriptures indicate that Christians are also to love *all* fellow humans and not only Christians. Peter's point focused on how believers could and should live out their continual interaction with fellow believers. Having love as the first thing on the heart's agenda is a matter of priority and necessity for the Christian.

Peter also brought in the how of that love. Consider how the body of Christ is filled with a myriad of differences: body types, ages, looks, backgrounds, personalities, abilities, quirks—you name it. Also consider that back in early church times, Christians had constant exposure to one another as they gathered daily in the temple and ate together from house to house. That was a lot of closeness among a variety of personalities. To me, it's a marvel that with such daily close exposure, coupled with the various quirks of individuals, their activities were done with "gladness and sincerity of heart" (Acts 2:46). It makes one wonder about that pithy statement familiarity breeds contempt. Well, it can, even in the church, as we shall see.

We can only surmise how long this lovefest lasted, but it doesn't take long for Bible accounts to reveal problems between believers (See Acts 5:1-10, 6:1-6). These developing problems continued to exist and increased, belying the church's idyllic beginning. Some twenty years after the Acts 2 account of the early Christians' "gladness and sincerity of heart" experience, Peter penned his words in 1 Peter 4:8 about the need for Christians to grow or stretch their love for one another. Was Peter identifying the love failure among God's people or at least among a number of believers? Whatever his reason, he called to account all believers with these important words: "Above all, have fervent love one for another, because love covers a multitude of sins" (1 Peter 4:8).

Since the body of Christ is so diverse in its makeup, people have to learn to get along with others who are quite different from them. The same is true in marriage. I think it's worth noting that although a multitude of sins might be covered by stretching one's love, perhaps not all sins fit under the covering. Particularly in a marriage context, if a spouse continually, carelessly, and willfully sins against a mate and takes advantage of the mate's covering of forgiveness, the offending mate may wear out his or her welcome.

It's true that Jesus said we are to forgive seventy times seven (See Matthew 18:22), which in a wooden type of translation would be an exact 490 times, but better understood, Jesus was speaking about the ongoing nature that forgiveness should have. Added to the mix for proper understanding, we must remember that forgiveness does not mean there is no consequence for wrongful action. If one breaks the law by harming another, the one who has been harmed may forgive the person who is guilty of the wrongful deed, but that forgiveness does not negate the call for recompense or consequence.

To love fervently is a must if we are to make life work as a Christian community and as couples joined in marriage. We are to have fervent love. The Greek word for *fervent* is *ektenes*. *Ek* means out, and *tenes* means stretch. [20] Put together, *ektenes* means to stretch out. The reason one needs to stretch one's love is found by considering the ongoing, explosive number of divorces in our country, including among Christians. The simple answer to so many broken marriages is that spouses feel they no longer love their spouses. They have run out of love (assuming there was love at the beginning). The legal term most commonly used as grounds for divorce in the courts is irreconcilable differences. That's another way of saying an individual or a couple have run of gas (love). Having nothing left, they have reached the end of their marital road.

When two people first marry, which might be considered the puppy love stage, there is not enough in the love tank to carry the couple through the up-and-down experiences over many years of marriage. No love reserves have been built to cover the times when there is a love shortage and down experiences test the relationship. Love tanks must be refilled—and expanded—if one is to experience a lasting marriage as God originally designed marriage to be. The Bible informs us that a multitude of sins committed in relationships is covered by continually stretching

---

[20] William Vine, "Fervent, Fervently," *Vine's Expository Dictionary of New Testament Words,* Blue Letter Bible, https://www.blueletterbible.org/search/Dictionary/viewTopic.cfm.

one's love. Note that the Bible passage deals with sins and not petty annoyances, irritations, or slights, even though it is reasonable to assume these are included. If as a Christian your love continues to mature, that growth will shape and enable you to handle the various offenses visited on you by others and most importantly, including your spouse.

In 1 Peter 4:8, the Greek word for *sins* is *hamartia*, which means to miss the mark.[21] More specifically, it means to miss God's mark or standard of holiness. How many times in my marriage have I missed God's mark of living out holiness when I've sinned against my wife? How many times have I not cherished her as I should? How many times did I speak harshly to her or feel annoyed? How often did I withhold compliments that I should have shared about or with her? How many times did I falsely accuse her of something? How many times was I unfair to her? Many, if not all, of these are sins against her. I missed God's mark of holiness in the midst of it all, and I will regretfully continue to do so as an imperfect man. However, biblically, I know Christ met God's requirement for holiness. By our faith and trust in Christ and by God's grace, holiness is placed within believers. It gives me hope that I can continue to grow and change, to the point of being a better husband day by day. Not a perfect husband, but a growing husband.

As the embodiment of God, Christ hit God's bull's-eye dead center. Once Christ declares us holy because of our faith, we are to display that holiness in practical ways, through our pursuits, conduct, and actions. As I have grown spiritually, the time between my marital failures has grown further and further apart, and the duration of my failures gets shorter and shorter. I appreciate the words of John Newton,[22] a former slave trader

---

[21] William Vine, "Sin (Noun and Verb)," *Vine's Expository Dictionary of New Testament Words,* Blue Letter Bible, https://www.blueletterbible.org/search/dictionary/viewtopic.cfm.

[22] *The Christian Spectator,* Vol. 3 (1821), 186.

who became a Christian and then a pastor. He penned the lyrics for perhaps the best-known Christian hymn, "Amazing Grace."

I am not what I ought to be. Ah, how imperfect and deficient I am. I am not what I wish to be. I abhor what is evil, and I cleave to what is good. I am not what I hope to be. Soon, soon, I shall put off mortality, and with mortality, all sin, and imperfection. Yet though I am not what I ought to be, wish to be, or hope to be, I can truly say that I am not what I once was—a slave of sin and Satan. I can heartily join with the apostle and acknowledge that by the grace of God, I am what I am.

As both my wife and I continue to grow and experience positive change, the fruit we enjoy is a thriving marriage. I pray the same for you.

Keep Stretching!

Having benchmarks or goals you can shoot for helps stretch your love. I have learned to consciously look for ways I can demonstrate my love for my wife, which is not what I did in the earlier part of my marriage. When looking back to those early years together with my wife and in seeing myself in the mirror of marriage, I realize that like numerous men I have known, I simply let marriage happen. I lived daily without much thought of the effort I needed to put forth to make my marriage what it ought to be. I simply thought one took marriage as it came, and that meant letting marriage take care of itself. Marriage did not and does not take care of itself. Many individuals are dying on the vine in their marriages due to their spouse's inattention to the responsibilities of marriage, and ultimately, to their mates. Marriage needs to be nurtured and worked on like any field one hopes to receive a harvest from. As the Bible declares, we will reap what we sow (See Galatians 6:7).

I once heard a humorous yet sad story of a counseling situation between a husband and wife who had been married for more than fifty years. Her complaint, which brought them into marriage counseling, was that she felt her husband didn't love her, for he rarely said he loved her throughout their marriage. She only remembered hearing it once—and that was when he proposed. The counselor quizzed the husband, asking, "Do you love your wife?"

"Yep!" came a gruff reply from the former marine.

The counselor asked, "Do you ever tell her you love her?"

Back came the reply, "Yep. I told her the day I proposed, and if anything changed, I would let her know!"

In marriage, one time will not cut it. If you want to stretch your love, you must grow in your knowledge about the right things to do and follow through with them. You must do them *to, for,* and *with* your mate. Even telling your sweetheart you love him or her is not enough, for you must also show and grow love to the point that the recipient feels secure in it.

The best professional sports players in the world have a mindset that seeks improvement virtually every day. Practice, practice, and practice are three keywords that sum up the hope for success, even for the most talented players. Along with their exceptional talent, some athletes put in the time and effort to improve. These are the people who usually rise to the top. They have understood that talent alone will not take them there. Motivation, drive, and lifestyle are critical elements in an athlete's world of success and longevity. The business world is forever offering seminars to help keep their employees sharp, growing, and on the cutting edge of technology. In the sports or business world, stretching one's abilities while seeking the next level is a key component of success. Such activity allows one to reach the top and stay there.

The same is true of the Christian life. We read in 2 Peter 1:5–8,

> Now for this very reason also, applying all diligence, in your faith supply moral excellence,

and in *your* moral excellence, knowledge, and in *your* knowledge, self-control, and in *your* self-control, perseverance, and in *your* perseverance, godliness, and in *your* godliness, brotherly kindness, and in *your* brotherly kindness, love. For if these *qualities* are yours and are increasing, they render you neither useless nor unfruitful in the true knowledge of our Lord Jesus Christ.

This dedication to spiritual and character growth is likewise needed for a solid marriage of the God variety. We are to strive for a successful marriage, for it will not be handed to us. We cannot have the product without going through the process. Make the commitment and enroll in the process. Purposefully tell and show your mate how much you love him or her.

What has the marriage mirror reflected back to you about your efforts or lack thereof in this area of commitment to growth in your marriage and your spouse? Write down any ideas you may have where you could and should exert new efforts to stretch your love. It may not be too late for you to experience marriage as it should and can be.

CHAPTER 11

Blindness

MEN ARE NOTORIOUS FOR NOT reading (or following) directions. "I don't need them," we say. An hour later, we still do not need them, despite the fact that the project isn't progressing but actually regressing. We will have to spend time undoing what we wrongly assembled before we again start the process. Our pride and stubbornness as men make us quite a piece of work, but women can prove to be equally stubborn.

My wife and I certainly have had our battle of wills on numerous occasions. One day when we were newly married, I got sick, so I asked my wife to go to the corner Peoples Drug Store, which was two blocks away, to get some medicine. She agreed to go but casually interjected a correction, saying it was Dart Drug and not Peoples. I was insistent that it was Peoples Drug, and she was just as adamant that it was Dart Drug. It was a light argument that went on for about five minutes. Then despite being sick, I challenged her by saying that we would both go (so that I could enjoy seeing her response when proven wrong). We both went, convinced that the other person was wrong, and found that neither of us was correct—it was Drug Fair. We both ate crow that day, yet neither of us yet learned the lesson in humility that we needed for a successful marriage. It would take more headbutting to get us to finally wake up and smell the roses (and avoid the thorns).

Who's Right?

While conducting counseling sessions, I have heard the complaints and explanations of people who were blind in their conversations. For example, a frustrated mate, whom we'll name John, was speaking to his spouse, whom we'll call Cindy, in front of me. During the discussion, I watched and listened as John tried to explain an issue to Cindy. I saw and heard John getting frustrated and agitated at Cindy because according to him, Cindy, as usual, was misconstruing things. I entered the fray and verified that Cindy had heard correctly, for I had also heard the exact thing. John denied that was what he said. After some mild debate and pushback on my part, John reluctantly recanted, by saying, "But that's not what I meant, and she should have known that!" That may not have been what John meant, but that was exactly what came across to his wife and me as I sat there listening.

It happens the other way around, too, where the wife speaks and then gets frustrated with what she concludes to be a husband who listens poorly. This scenario often plays out in a marriage where understandings are skewed, and the mistaken party does not own or acknowledge guilt.

In my marriage, I have often thought I was right in what I said and in my conclusion of what I thought my wife heard, only later to find I was wrong. Frequently, my wife has spoken things to me that I have heard wrongly, or she conveyed wrongly. It is never-ending. My wife's misunderstanding would get me so frustrated (a cousin of anger) at times that I was determined to tape our conversations to prove I was right. I never got around to doing any taping (and I probably should be glad I didn't), but there were times when I would humorously (so I say) appeal to our young children and pull them into our friendly discussions when I wanted them to support my recall of events. Sometimes I was proven right, and sometimes I was proven wrong. I have since learned to acknowledge my wrongs and apologize, as has my wife.

Throughout my years of marriage, I have learned that being right is not really that important in the grand scheme of things. Additionally, arguing is useless because there is no practical way to continually verify anyone's rightness in his or her recall, nor should it be a priority. Over the years, my wife and I have been wrong on many occasions. We have individually and collectively eaten crow so often that needing to be right has proven not to be a worthy pursuit. We have learned to let go of our need to be right; rather, we focus on living another day, letting things go that could divide, and loving each other in things that unite.

When there are many words, transgression is unavoidable, but he who restrains his lips is wise.

(Proverbs 10:19).

I've made up my version of this verse: Where there are many words, crossing the line into sin (transgression) is unavoidable; therefore, abandon the quarrel before it breaks out. Here is a tongue-in-cheek story. A husband got fired from his job. The discouraged husband sat with his wife while recounting his numerous setbacks in life, but in his discouragement, he also wanted to thank her for being there in his times of need, for there were plenty.

"When I was fired from my first job, you were there, sweetheart, right by my side. And again, when I got fired from a second job and then from another, you were always there beside me. Honey, when I fell off the ladder and broke my collarbone, again, you were there and drove me to the doctor. When I backed the car into a telephone pole and hurt my neck, again, you were right there by my side, and you drove me to the hospital." Then he goes quiet and looks away. Glancing back at his wife, he spoke with a slight frown now on his face. "You know, thinking on it, in all those moments when bad things happened to me, you were always right there beside me, every time. It just dawned on me; you must be the problem!"

He couldn't have gotten fired multiple times because he was a bad worker. He couldn't have fallen from the ladder because he was careless. He couldn't have backed into the telephone pole because he was an inattentive driver. Nothing's on him, so he thinks. Everything wrong in his life is on someone else. Who's most convenient? The spouse! In marriage, we can be so blind to ourselves that all of our wrongs are shifted, explained away, or reassigned to the closest scapegoat—our spouse.

Rather than getting into the long arguments or lengthy explanations that Joni and I once had over what was or was not said or who was or was not to blame, we have learned to strive to be gracious in our interactions. Now when there's disagreement over something, the hearer will kindly say something like, "I'm sorry. That's not what I heard. This is what I heard or understood you to say."

The initial speaker will respond, "I'm sorry I must not have been clear about what I said or asked. Let me restate it." We continue to learn to give and receive grace (and clarity) in marriage. Do we do it every time? No. Do we do it perfectly? No.

Can You See?

Mental blindness can keep people from walking away from issues when they should; rather, it provokes them to gear up for battle. Such blindness can be harmful in virtually all of life's venues, but it is devastating in a marriage. Where does this blindness come from? It comes from the wrong kind of pride. People can have positive pride in jobs well done. Yet these same people can have destructive pride, which is birthed in self-sufficiency. They see themselves as the standard in life. Fallen pride keeps spouses from embracing the very help that a couple needs and can find in each other, which God created and fashioned for their mutual benefit.

When a husband is blind and shuts out his wife's counsel and help, he shoots himself in the foot. When he does not love and listen to her as he should, he creates a resistant spirit and tension within their marriage. She may counter by fighting for his love and attention and end up inadvertently being against him because of his stubborn pride. This is also true of the wife who shuts down her husband.

In the Ray Stevens's song "Everything Is Beautiful," we find the lyrics, "There is none so blind as he who will not see."[23] This is an interesting song and message sung by a man who is physically blind. Husbands, are you so blind mentally, or emotionally, or spiritually in your relationship with your wife that you either cannot or will not see what your pride and stubbornness are doing to you, your wife, your marriage, and your family? Why won't you go to counseling? Why won't you ask or accept her input or help from others? Why won't you humble yourself and apologize? Why do you choose to argue with her rather than put your arms around her and show her that nothing will come between you, her, and your love for her? Why won't you acknowledge and appreciate her help? Some men are so stubborn and prideful that it takes the hard knocks of life to get their attention. Sometimes those knocks come too late. As the Bible warns, pride precedes a fall (See Proverbs 16:18). Shutting down or out a spouse may result in the sounds of silence within a marriage. Those sounds of silence can intensify and become deafening.

For you wives who are reading, how blind have you been to the gem of a husband you have? Granted, he is not everything you may want him to now be. Are you blind because you choose to focus on all you don't have in him, or will you change your view and focus on what you *do* have in him? Stop comparing him to other men, but rather, take what you have and learn to enjoy him, as you want him to enjoy you. If you believe he is a partner pursuing a good-faith marriage, even as you are, then focus on the bigger prize—learning to be a happy couple while possessing a fallen nature and living in a fallen world where nothing is perfect.

---

[23] Ray Stevens, "Everything is Beautiful," Genius.com, https://genius.com/Ray-stevens-everything-is-beautiful-lyrics.

As you again look into the marriage mirror, it's time to linger a little longer and carefully consider if there might be some blind spots that you may have been overlooking in yourself.

Think on what your spouse sees in you when he or she looks into your face. Realize, your face is also a mirror that reflects to others what's inside you. Does your spouse see a face of acceptance looking back at them, a face of love and warmth, or does your spouse look into a face of disappointment and tolerance looking back at them? Ask God by whatever means needed to open your eyes as to how you are truly viewed by those you love. Act positively on what is revealed to you.

CHAPTER 12

Minutiae in Marriage

Minutiae: very small details.[24]

WE KNOW THE BIG-TICKET ITEMS that can destroy a marriage, such as a mate committing adultery, marital abuse, or the devastating effects of sinful anger and a temper. But what about small-ticket items? Can they also affect whether or not a marriage will last and how happy it may or may not be? They absolutely can.

The little foxes, that spoil the vines. (Song of Solomon 2:15 KJV)

> In Samuel Martin's book *Rain upon the Mown Grass, and Other Sermons*, he notes, Foxes are exceedingly destructive to both the yield and the producer of the fruit. By the action of their teeth on the bark they destroy the vine, and by their voracious appetite they devour much of the fruit. Making matters worse, they do not roam as do other animals that would minimize their damage, for they fix the bounds of their habitation at a convenient

---

[24] · *Oxford American Dictionary, Heald Colleges Edition* (New York: Oxford University Press, 1980).

distance near their choice of plunder. The breadth of their mischief and their cunning renders defenses almost useless. [25]

Little Foxes in a Marriage

This verse about little foxes spoiling the vines appears to be speaking of a bride expressing concern to her groom over the potentially harmful little foxes that could endanger their relationship and marriage. While applying this principle, maintaining relationships on any level will require attention to detail if those relationships are to remain healthy and lasting. This is particularly true of marriage because marriage is unique in its composition.

Some think that marriage is analogous to having a roommate, and in some ways that may be true, but the two experiences obviously differ. Although living with a roommate can prove advantageous, like marriage, it can also be complicated and stressful. In marriage, stress and complications cannot be as easily mitigated as one might do with a roommate. With a roommate, one is better able to control contact and damaging iteration, get a break as needed, or manipulate a schedule enough to have limited interaction. And in a worst-case scenario, one may choose to move.

This is not easily done with a marriage partner, where two lives are deeply intertwined. The day-in and day-out exposure in married life coupled with the marital commitment expected from each spouse can keep you in constant contact with your partner. You may get pockets of separation from time to time, but those are often short-lived in the grand scheme of things. As a married couple, there can be a lot of togetherness: sleeping, eating, planning, worshiping, vacationing, holidays, having children,

---

[25] Samuel Martin, "The Little Foxes," *Rain upon the Mown Grass and Other Sermons 1842-1870* (London: Hodder and Stoughton, 1871), 43.

arguing, and sharing friends are but a few possible life routines of married partners. You are bound together, warts and all.

Little annoyances that crop up in such constant exposure to each other can lead to big gaps in a relationship if they are allowed to grow and fester. When one marries, the proverbial example of leaving the cap off the toothpaste is humorously cited for portending trouble ahead. Although neither my wife nor I leave the cap off the toothpaste, we each would have mountains to conquer if we had allowed molehills to grow.

My wife had the habit of leaving the vacuum cleaner in the middle of a doorway when she was distracted by interruptions and forgot to finish the job and put the vacuum away. In haste and assuming my pathway to be clear, half paying attention while walking I turned the corner to enter a room and stumbled over an abandoned vacuum cleaner. It was an irritation for me. "I'm sorry; I didn't mean to do that," she explained when investigating the thud that she had heard when I had stumbled. She had planned to return and finish the job, but she had forgotten and moved on to other things. Over the years, she has worked on that issue and greatly improved her consideration of me.

I had the habit of not finishing work projects at home. I allowed my tools to linger at a work site, which made my lack of promptly completing tasks difficult for my wife. She either had to pick up my tools to get them out of the way or work around them when cleaning. This was annoying for her. "I'm sorry; I didn't mean to do that," would be my words. Then I would explain how it was easier for me to leave the tools there. It allowed for quick resumption when picking up where I had left off, as time became available. Over time, I have worked on this lack of consideration for her and greatly improved by cleaning up each time, even though it was a pain because I was not yet finished with the project. I could cite other "foxes" my wife had, as I could about my own, but you and your spouse have enough of your own to think about.

The question to ask is what should you do about those destructive little foxes that can gnaw away at your marriage? Left unattended, those little foxes can grow into larger foxes.

1. The first step is to *acknowledge* that over time, *you* bring foxes into the marriage as much as your mate does. Those ongoing habits of nitpicking can become very annoying, irritating, and divisive to a partner. Resist the temptation to believe your mate's foxes are bigger and more numerous than your own.

2. Identify and own the irritations, annoyances, and idiosyncrasies that you bring to the marriage. Identify any of your actions that appear upsetting to your mate: words or phrases that can appear to be argumentative or nonverbal expressions and reactions that can be offensive. Some examples are rolling the eyes in response to your mate's words, a half-smile or slight smirk that conveys a belittling spirit, a slight shaking of the head in a disapproving manner, or engaging in something that distracts you while your mate is trying to converse with you.

3. Ask your mate if you display any irritating idiosyncrasies or annoyances that he or she identifies as bothersome. When your partner identifies something in you, be careful not to explain away, excuse, or rationalize your behavior. Rather, just listen.

4. Now that you are aware of the irritations you bring, the fourth step is letting your mate know you will work to overcome or at least mitigate them. To help you, ask your mate to kindly call you on it when you display annoying or irritating actions or to bring it to your attention later at an established airing-out-your-marriage evaluation time (Number 25, Appendix 1: The Twenty-Five *A*'s of an Awesome Marriage).

5. Express appreciation to your mate when you see him or her exert effort to change habits that hurt you or the relationship.

The secret to engaging in marriage as it ought to be is for each mate to change and grow so that offenses occur with less redundancy and impact. They become fewer and further between. As a bonus, when a spouse witnesses a partner's positive efforts at change, it positively impacts the observer.

Fox Denial

Another aspect that couples need to address concerns those dreaded foxes in marriage, which I call *fox denial*. This is when one mate sees a fox in the marriage vineyard slowly gnawing away at the marriage. The other partner does not see it or denies it is there.

A case in point is our kitchen refrigerator. I am convinced that my wife sometimes unknowingly sabotages the refrigerator so that things fall out when I open the door. My reflexes go into motion, but some items slip through the sure hands of this former baseball catcher and end up on the kitchen floor, sometimes splattered in a mess, which I clean up while quietly grumbling. My wife denies any claim of sabotage and offers her innocent assessment. She says that perhaps I'm not careful enough when I open the door. Her explanation is not spoken maliciously to me, but many times she speaks in half-jest. I think she doesn't realize the precarious way she sometimes puts things back in the refrigerator when she is in a hurry.

One fox I used to deny existing in me was more serious than a booby-trapped refrigerator. During my young ministry years, I drove my budding family to church, parked, immediately sprang from the car, and headed into the church building. All the while, I greeted people along the way as I moved into the church building and on to my ministry responsibilities. I was oblivious to the wife I left behind. She struggled as a new mother, fending for herself while gathering up a small child, a diaper bag, and personal belongings. My insensitivity and shortsightedness during those early days was a festering molehill, which could have grown into a potential mountain of hurt inside my wife. Thankfully, I awoke in time to recognize that I had a dutiful but unhappy wife, and I made the necessary changes.

Little things in marriage that hurt and offend can grow and take on a life of their own. If I had not had an awakening moment over my insensitivity to my wife's plight as a young mother, resentment could easily have festered within her to the point of no return.

So how do you handle the issues you see in your marriage that your mate does not? What do you do when their existence is denied? Let me answer by first addressing an important balancing principle in the marriage dynamic. A major premise of this book is to look at oneself in the mirror of marriage and work on oneself, to have the best chance to achieve the successful marriage you want. Does this mean you are never allowed to address any shortcomings on your partner's part that affect your marriage? No, as hopefully you saw from earlier passages in this book. Marriage is a two-way street, so you *should* address issues in your spouse that can be divisive to a marriage, but it is critical to do it in the right way and at the right time so that you do not inflict added stress on a marriage and no issue takes on a life of its own.

When you believe something needs to be addressed concerning your partner's wrongful actions or inaction, it is important to approach respectfully and as an appeal. For example, do not attack your partner with accusations based on your feelings or thoughts, which may have no factual merit. You cannot (should not) tell your partner what he or she thinks. You can tell your partner the way some action or inaction on his or her part contributes to the way you feel, how it came across to you, or how something appears to be, but you are not clairvoyant. Once you bring up an issue about your partner, and you are sure that your partner has heard you, leave it there and avoid the temptation to iterate and reiterate. At this stage, you must trust the Lord to work in your mate as you continue to work on yourself in light of what God is showing you (See 1 Peter 2:23). God gives you direction through His Word, in prayer, through personal conviction and conscience, from other people, or by circumstances in life.

If you keep matters in your own hands and decide to constantly revisit (uninvited) sensitive and sore issues against your mate, there will be trouble in your marriage, and strife will increase in the relationship. If you continually nag or push, you may or may not get what you want, but in the process, don't be surprised if your spouse emotionally or even physically moves away from you. Your best hope in solving your issues will not come by nagging or pushing, regardless of whether it is the husband or wife is doing it.

If your mate is pulling or has pulled away due to certain behaviors you display, pushing matters will only worsen the situation if either spouse continues the practice. To replace displays of damaging behaviors, try rebuilding the relationship by identifying places, times, or events where you can take advantage of togetherness. When riding together in a car, reach over, take your spouse's hand, and hold it, not so that it becomes uncomfortable but long enough to let your mate know you're reaching out for connection. When walking together, reach out and take your partner's hand or put your arm around his or her waist. Do not wait for your partner to do it. You do it. You may want your partner to be the first to engage so that you will know your partner wants it, but do not wait for that to happen. Take a risk, let love take action, and hopefully, your gesture will promote a positive reaction. A steady diet of little annoyances, irritations, and idiosyncrasies can gnaw away at and damage marital relationships. Conversely, small matters of affection, attention, and intentionality can add up in a big way to turn around a marriage.

To one who knows the right thing to do and does not do it, for him it is sin. (James 4:17).

My wife and I have grown, and we have chosen to try to positively affect each other. As an example, let's go back to the refrigerator. While sitting at the kitchen counter, I noticed that the refrigerator door was slightly ajar after my wife thought she had closed it as she left the kitchen. It can be a little difficult to tell when the refrigerator door is fully closed, so it takes a little extra care to ensure the door is shut. I walked over and closed the door. Later while together again in the kitchen, I said, "Sweetheart, just as a note, the refrigerator door wasn't fully closed when you left."

She graciously responded, "I'm glad you're around to look after me." For the record, she wasn't being sarcastic. If I were to have discovered the door slightly ajar in the early stages of our marriage, I would have said, "Joni, you *have* to make sure the door is shut, or we will have spoiled food. How many times do I have to tell you?"

She would have replied, "What about you? You're not careful in some things too."

Grateful for Growth

At this juncture, I give you a sobering thought. In my counseling experience I have found far more marriages have succumbed to foxes than to the bigger ticket items first mentioned in this chapter. To be forewarned is to be forearmed.

I am so grateful for the growth in both of us. It has allowed us to advance and keep moving our marriage deeper and deeper into positive ground. Joni has been just as gracious to me when I have faltered in something, and she calls my attention to it. Joni and I don't call each other out like we used to over inadvertent missteps, for we have learned to maturely measure our words and responses to each other. Do we do it perfectly every time? No.

In marriage, the things that first attract you may later repel you. I have found that when a couple marries, a mate may be happy with the laid-back nature of his or her partner. This quality may have originally drawn the mate to the partner. Let's fast-forward to years later. That laid-back spirit may now be interpreted by the irritated spouse as a couldn't-care-less attitude in regard to important things, and both spouses take offense if the issue is discussed.

Unless both spouses work on evicting the foxes of offense or coming to a reasonable compromise over differing perspectives, emotional and physical distance can result. As you continue to see yourself in the mirror of marriage, can you identify the little irritants, annoyances, and idiosyncrasies in you, which might cause negative reactions in your mate, that you need to let go of?

Evaluate the legitimacy of your spouse's reactions. Just because your spouse gets annoyed at you does not mean the annoyance has justifiable merit. Perhaps in the offended mind it has merit, but not necessarily legitimacy. The purpose of this reflective moment is not to beat yourself up or suggest that you must change yourself in accordance with whatever your spouse thinks or wants. The idea is to be as honest as you can with yourself and act on what you deem to be a legitimate need for change in yourself to better your marriage.

It's time again for that reflection check. To discern minutiae matters, it will require getting a little closer to the mirror, or brightening the light. Consider from this chapter the smallest things you might do in your marriage that are annoying to your spouse, Let your spouse know that your eyes have been open about yourself and that you will be working on correcting that irritant. Remember, little issues can gnaw away at the marriage bond.

CHAPTER 13

Impasse

AYO IS A MIDDLE-AGED DOCTOR, who will soon be made a partner in an established practice. He hails from an African nation. His wife, Maria, comes from a country in the Far East. She is a working mother, both inside and outside the home. Her mother lives with them and helps with childcare and chores in the home.

Coming from an African background, he was reared in a sharing culture, where nothing was held onto tightly, and people did not claim much as their own. Family was viewed as more than just blood. The whole community opened their hearts and embraced everyone as their own. On the other hand, his wife came from a background where she and her family had little. There wasn't much they could afford to share, so it was important to hang onto and treat carefully whatever they could secure. Both are high-quality godly people, who have allowed me to tell their story and include it in this book. Their names have been changed.

After the wedding, she willingly set aside her career dreams to support her husband's efforts to become a medical doctor. After years of study and sacrifice, Ayo secured a medical diploma, and they were ready to settle down. Years of renting had left both desiring a house they could call their own. For their growing family, she wanted a larger house than he thought they could afford. Even though he was leery of the purchase, he went along with her choice. When she thought about financially affording the house, she considered his financial track record, which was not good. In her thinking, the money was there, but the way he spent the money was a roadblock. Ever since she had known him, he had been a giver and a man who had freely shared what he had with others. Perhaps he had sometimes given others more than he should have, to his detriment, but that giving mindset had been imbedded within him by his culture.

Being the more frugal one but also a generous giver in her own right, she was confident that the money was there, but he would need to adjust his ways and put his family first in providing for them. Adding to the issue, she was working, earning money, and contributing financially to the cause, but she now withheld her money and kept it separate from the family pot. When she combined her money with his income, there was enough to cover the bills, with a little extra left over. Somehow the extra went out the door (guess by whom) and into the hands of others, but they were worthy causes, in most cases.

In a nutshell, what were the problems? The husband had allowed himself to be too independent of his wife. As a husband, he was to cleave or cling to his wife. This meant nothing was to come between them, be it their children, relatives, or lifestyles. Into the marriage, he brought a lifestyle he allowed to come between him and his wife. Into the home, she brought the problem of insecurity from her childhood, and it played out in her need for and use of control.

Rather than the wife keeping her money separately, he wanted them to combine their earnings as they used to. Why had that practice stopped? In addition to his being a very giving person, he had also not spent wisely in a number of business transactions. He had lost money, which included her money. At that point, she didn't feel she could fully trust his financial judgments. This fed her feelings of insecurity, which harkened back to the poverty of her childhood days. From her perspective, she had not kept her earnings and spent them on herself. She had contributed to family obligations, which she had protected, to ensure the children would have piano lessons and other such opportunities. In the past when they had combined their monies, there never seemed to be enough left over to support the activities both had wanted their children to enjoy. She didn't want to have separate finances, but she felt it was the only way she could ensure that they would meet their desires for their children.

What does a couple do when they are stuck on an issue, and they cannot reach a point of resolution? Each side believes it has a legitimate argument. Compromise is virtually impossible because the legitimate argument to one person is not legitimate to the other. What was the solution? Some counselors would direct the wife to be submissive to the husband, do as he wished, combine their incomes, and trust God to work in his heart. In my earlier years of counseling, that would have been my suggestion, but I now see it differently. If the wife was made to be a helpmeet—and she was and is—what would be the best way to help her husband?

Relationship Determines Response

While I was a youth pastor for ten years, I learned a lesson about effective ministry to teenagers. I learned that the relationship I had with each teenager determined the response I would have from each one. From this insight, I coined the phrase, "Relationship determines response." I have found that this truth applies across the board to most, if not all, interactions with people, especially with one's marriage partner.

In the counseling case that I cited in this chapter, the relationship, which had a touch of tension, would not be repaired until the husband earned back his wife's trust. He had forfeited it by earlier arbitrary decisions. He believed that he had learned his lesson from his prior mistakes, and she should now trust him, but it was not that easy. The key for him to earn back her trust was to give up his independent ways and develop a track record of interacting with her more in the decision-making process. This was what she yearned for, rather than his going off and following his independent ideas, as he has done in the past.

What did she need to do? She needed to learn to overcome her insecurity because it showed up in her marriage in other ways. Her insecurity constantly bred the need to be in control. When her husband proved himself to be financially sound, she might find it difficult to give up her control and partner with him in combining the funds. Both husband and wife needed to sit down and come up with a plan that had benchmarks along the way and that recognized his positive changes, which in turn, would allow her to alter her need to guard her finances.

As I counseled them, each had a laundry list of inconsistencies they saw in the arguments of the other. He preferred a smaller home with a smaller mortgage, which would leave enough money each month to build up savings and a rainy-day fund. Because she knew him, she shared all the reasons why that would not happen. When the wife shared her reasons for how she operated and what she wanted, the husband was there to counter his assessment of her thinking and plans.

I tried to help them see that each person in a relationship can point out the inconsistencies, hypocrisy, and fallacies in the other person's perspective, which we all have, but few can recognize and acknowledge his or her own foibles. Each person believes that he or she sees and thinks clearly about himself or herself, but it is hard to do that from another person's perspective.

Until this husband earned back his wife's trust, she would continue to battle the anxiety that insecurity brought and struggle with giving up control. Being the head of the home and his wife, it was incumbent on him as the servant leader to wisely and lovingly provoke the impetus in his wife to change. She wanted it to be different—as it ought to be—and he was the one who could make it happen. Coming to a compromise seemed to be the best solution. But was it possible?

Choosing to Compromise

To some, compromise is a non-option, for they are stubbornly wise in their own eyes, set in their own ways, and not interested in accommodating another person's point of view. Others dislike compromise because they feel it is a lose-lose proposition. Although compromise seems fair, those who view it as losing have difficulty accepting the part that they lost. So where does that leave a couple?

Ultimately, three options are available for settling an impasse. Obviously before making your choice, you want to rethink and revisit an issue, but it will boil down to choosing one of the following three options.

1. First, there is the art of compromise, in which both individuals get an acceptable portion while living with what they had to give up to satisfy the other spouse.
2. Second, there is the option of continuing to live in a state of argument and stalemate, which can breed ongoing battles over unsettled issues or result in decisions that are left dangling.
3. Third, there is the option where one mate, usually the dominant one, runs roughshod over the other and does as he or she pleases. I believe this often happens in marriages.

I have found that the person who is most likely to break an impasse over unresolved issues is the one who cares the most about having a happy, lasting, and successful marriage. But let me give a warning. The person who constantly bears the weight of breaking impasses by deferring to the other may eventually tire of doing so. In those cases, that person may be molded into a formidable opponent against the one who allows such inequity to exist. Such a marriage may survive, but it will not thrive.

If you are a smart husband and wife (partners), you will prioritize and learn the art of compromise, in which both win an acceptable percentage of what they want. Some readers might object to my use of a winning and losing concept when explaining compromise in a marriage setting. If you and your spouse can compromise without having a winning/losing mentality, you are to be commended. In my counseling findings, it is difficult for many couples to achieve, simply because so many of the issues requiring compromise can be highly charged. One or both parties believe that each needs to win on this issue. Certain issues become the hill to die on, making compromise hard to swallow and virtually impossible to achieve, especially when both are vying for that same hill.

For most of us, the situations needing compromise are of the everyday garden variety, in which various levels of give and take succeed. This allows each a reasonable level of satisfaction. But surfacing occasionally are those instances where one wants a clear and unadulterated win—a *full* win to enjoy. That's my wife and me (more me). These times are fewer and further between than the garden variety of compromises, but they are pure heaven when it is one's turn to win.

Let me give you an example. My wife enjoys vacationing in settled spots, where we stay for a week or so in a geographical region and explore. I like to vacation in large swaths, such as a week or two of cross-country-type driving. We have settled on the plan that we do one vacation trip her way and another trip my way. Some trips are a combination of both ways. For me, a pure win is a time of driving, driving, driving, and seeing sights along the way—not staying too long in any one place. That is one of my favorite kinds of vacations. We recently completed a five-day vacation that covered 1,735 miles and six states. Her way to vacation is spending a whole week at the beach—the whole week, the whole beach, and nothing but the beach.

Now, let's talk about the elephant in the room. What happens when the impasse remains an impasse, and there is no compromise? You, as a couple, must ask yourselves about your motive in holding out. Are you being immature, stubborn, or ignorant about the facts on the issue causing the impasse? Is the issue truly a hill to die on, and if you determine that it is so, how will your unyielding position affect your marriage? (Be careful; if there are too many hills you choose to die on, your marriage may not recover). Have you solicited the views or insights of others regarding their take on the impasse or to help break the impasse? Ask, "Who gets their way more often in relationship decisions?" and then consider the appropriate action to take in light of the answer. Can you agree on a trade-off or flip a coin, where one spouse is deferred to in the present impasse, and the conceding spouse's choice takes precedence if there is another impasse? If you have tried all avenues of resolution and an impasse still remains, each will have to accept and learn to live with what is and the fallout that accumulates from unresolved impasses. Be warned that there will be fallout that may be lasting.

Look at impasses and compromises. Seeing yourself in the mirror of marriage will require a hard look at yourself. Truth be told, most often, we all think we are right in our views and determinations. You and I know how hard it is to defer to the views of another when perspectives are different. It proves to be especially hard in a marriage relationship. Why? Because there has been so much back and forth in discussions and debates over so many issues for such an ongoing period in marriage that each spouse has witnessed his or her mate's fallibilities in assessments, conclusions, and reasoning over issues. That revelation about both spouses can undercut full trust in what your spouse says or thinks about things. At times, your spouse has been wrong about things. This has also been true about you. But too often, the focus on past wrongs is what you think is true about your spouse and not yourself. Therefore, you tend to trust yourself more than trusting your spouse.

Regarding compromise, each spouse has his or her own perspective and set of facts. To compromise does not mean you have to be convinced and swayed to your spouse's arguments or point of view. It means you respect your spouse's perspective and that you will accept or accommodate his or her desires by being fair and taking turns. This assumes that you trust your mate and that if you can't accept and respect your spouse's opinion and subsequent choices, trust issues lie at the bottom of your inability or unwillingness to compromise. Then times of impasse become more probable in your marriage. Check yourself: If a compromise is very hard for you, consider why that is true and discuss it with your spouse.

Some would argue that any impasse in a marriage and family is broken by the head, meaning the man makes the ultimate decision. Before you go there, husbands, you need to ask what loving your wife as Christ loved the church looks like and in a practical way. You must also visit Peter's instruction in 1 Peter 5:7, where husbands are called upon to grant their wives honor as fellow heirs of the grace of life. I would remind all Christian husbands that godly headship is about leading in the *demonstration* of servanthood. It is not as simple as the husband's right to the last word on matters.

Looking into the mirror, do you see yourself viewing your spouse as a stubborn, unyielding individual across the table, or do you see a spouse who wants to do right by you? Can you take any serious and unresolved issues to other people so that you can gain clarity and insight if the impasse is of high consequence? If the impasse is not of such high importance to be taken to another older and wiser person for input, but it's more of garden variety issues, a lack of compromise among married partners is rooted in something else, namely, pride or stubbornness.

CHAPTER 14

Dr. Jekyll and Mr. Hyde

AS YOU WORKED THROUGH THIS book, hopefully you have begun seeing yourself in the mirror of marriage while trying to ascertain shortcomings within yourself, with the expectation that uncovering those flaws might lead to avoiding the actions or inactions that sabotage a marriage. From there, we began including more of the *we* part of a marriage, where each spouse needed to examine how he or she impacted the other while intertwining their lives. Then I addressed difficulties that may arise between spouses in the form of foxes and impasses. Now, we move into an arena that is most difficult for an unsuspecting spouse to live in, but sadly, so many do. It is living in a Jekyll and Hyde environment foisted upon one spouse by the other.

If you are the victim living in such a household, as you look into the mirror of marriage you may find you don't really recognize yourself anymore, for you look quite different than you remember yourself to look. Living with a Jekyll and Hyde spouse can sap you of being you. You walk on eggshells, always aware that the most innocent thing can trigger your spouse to his dark side. How are you then to live?

I met Dr. Jekyll. As a matter of fact, I have met many Dr. Jekylls. I have worshiped with them while attending the same church. I was even teammates with them on some ball teams. I have worked with them on church projects. I have sat across a counseling table from some in my office. I have sat in their homes and counseled them at their dining room tables or in their living rooms. I have had glimpses of Mr. Hyde from time to time, but I have never met him directly—until I did, face-to-face. It was not pretty but rather, quite revealing and unsettling.

Dr. Jekyll and Mr. Hyde are the two main characters in an 1886 short novel by Robert Louis Stevenson. As you may know, these two characters are one person with two alter egos who exhibit wildly contradictory behavior—especially between their private and public selves. The actual title of the book is *The Strange Case of Dr. Jekyll and Mr. Hyde*.

If you met Dr. Jekyll, you likely would find him to be a very pleasant person, enjoyable to talk with, and perhaps even considered to be a friend. That's his charm. After all, he has many commendable personality traits. He may be a churchgoing and church-involved person with a public persona that cannot be questioned, for there is no reason to do so. When meeting Mr. Hyde, it is usually a secondhand introduction.

As a pastor, when a spouse of Dr. Jekyll comes in for counsel, and you hear about Mr. Hyde, it is hard to wrap your mind around what the spouse is saying because you have only known the one you are hearing about as Dr. Jekyll. In your thinking, there is a disconnect between what you are hearing and what you thought you knew about Dr. Jekyll. You do not know Mr. Hyde. In the spirit of trying to help, you reach out as a friend or pastor to Dr. Jekyll so that you can hear his side of the story about a serious marital issue brought to your attention. In short order as you converse with Dr. Jekyll, he begins hearing things from you that he doesn't want to hear. Dr. Jekyll starts to give way to Mr. Hyde.

It does not take long for a pastor to get on the wrong side of Mr. Hyde. Simply deny him what or how he thinks things should be, and you are well on the way there. As you talk and question him about what his spouse brought to you for counsel, he is insistent that he is Dr. Jekyll and that it is how he should be viewed. If there is a smattering of Mr. Hyde in him, it is only because his spouse creates such appearances. If she would honor, obey, and submit as he thinks she should, there would be no Mr. Hyde in her thinking. Those seeking to help will soon be in Mr. Hyde's crosshairs if the so-called helpers do not direct the wife to do what she ought to do, according to his determination. If she is leaving or has already left him, he reasons that she must return immediately and fulfill her Christian duty by submitting herself to this self-proclaimed God-fearing man.

If you are married to Dr. Jekyll and Mr. Hyde, you likely understand the source of his power. It is his use of cover, control, intimidation, and in many cases, the wallet. You will find that he will not easily relinquish any power he has. If his spouse wants to come out from under his tyranny, it will not be an easy task. Because of that, many women will not even try. Make no mistake. Plenty of wives have tried, but fear and doubt have beaten them back. A major part of Mr. Hyde's strength lies in his ability to intimidate.

Over the years, I have encountered Dr. Jekylls who were counterparts in occupational ministry who were gradually exposed as Mr. Hydes. I have counseled a number of women who have suffered in silence in their marriages to such ministers. When I met individually with those pastors to try to help through counseling, I was not welcomed into their world, to put it mildly. To them, the issue was cut and dried: The wife needed to learn to be submissive, which is how I should in my counseling be steering the wife.

Why Does the Wife Stay?

What causes the wife of a Dr. Jekyll to stay with a Mr. Hyde? There are a number of reasons, and one is because he is not always Mr. Hyde but also Dr. Jekyll. Dr. Jekyll has treated his wife well, and together, they have had many good times and made fond memories. Dr. Jekyll can be sweet, understanding, patient, kind, and loving—all the things a wife would want from a husband, and that initially drew her to him. She cannot deny his pleasant side. No one can, for it is there for all to see.

Remaining the wife of a Dr. Jekyll and Mr. Hyde plays itself out in various ways. A primary concern for the Christian wife is what the Lord would want. No godly wife would want to dishonor God, and by leaving the husband, she is fearful that she may be guilty of doing just that and destroying her husband's testimony or ministry. Other wives are simply afraid to make any move away from such husbands. It could be fear of retaliation from him or that she cannot make it alone. These wives stay and try to make the best of their situations by endeavoring to keep on the Dr. Jekyll side of the husband while tolerating any Mr. Hyde appearances.

Fear of failure will keep a wife in the Jekyll and Hyde home and marriage. She reasons, *I don't want to be part of a failed marriage*, for in her mind, there is a stigma attached to it. She may battle personal embarrassment as a wife who fears she may appear to others as one unable to make her marriage work. She assumes blame for the failure, especially since she is married to Dr. Jekyll, whom so many people view with the utmost respect. They think it highly unlikely that he would be the cause of any marital discord, so the fault must lie with her.

Some wives take the resigned route. There is no easy way out. How will they provide for themselves and their children? As much as they do not like Mr. Hyde, they still have Dr. Jekyll at least part of the time, and the children will not be uprooted. So they stay.

Other wives have settled into the combative route. They have put up with their husbands' split personalities for far too long. Feeling somewhat boxed in a corner with limited options in leaving, they feel forced to stay, so their only defense becomes a good offence, so they choose to battle back. The marriage may prove to be volatile, but neither one plans to give in, back down, or move on or out.

Then some wives leave. They have had their fill. They are determined to live in a sane world and leave the insanity behind. They finally recognize that they deserve more, have settled for too little for too long, and make a clean break. Fear is no longer allowed to be a dominant factor within them. They will not tolerate any longer being controlled by a dominating and volatile person.

I recently heard a talk by a woman who had been reared in a cult, and after years of being there, both she and her sister left it. Their other siblings and parents stayed. Even though she was no longer part of their lives and missed them dearly, she concluded, "The hardest day of freedom was better than the best day in a cult."[26] Like all cults, it employed mind-control techniques. Personal freedom and choice were virtually nonexistent, separation from outside contact was highly enforced, and the ability to walk away on one's own was extremely difficult, much like the situation the wife of Mr. Hyde faces. I hear some readers screaming, "But what about *Mrs.* Hyde!?! That's who I'm married to!"

Introducing Mrs. Jekyll and Mrs. Hyde

Unfortunately, I recognize that there is also a Mrs. Jekyll and Mrs. Hyde. Mrs. Hyde can be just as devastating as any male counterpart can be. Mrs. Hyde uses many of the same tactics, and husbands can fall prey to the same fears that abused wives face. So why did I choose to separate accounts about the Mr. Hydes and Mrs. Hydes? Because I have found that cases involving Mr. Hydes are perpetuated far more often than the other way around.

---

[26] Dawn Smith. "Why I Left an Evangelical Cult." TEDxNATICK video, https://www.ted.com/talks/dawn_smith_why_i_left_an_evangelical_cult/transcript.

As noted at the beginning of the chapter, the title of the Jekyll and Hyde story is *The Strange Case of Dr. Jekyll and Mr. Hyde.* It is strange indeed when one applies the Jekyll and Hyde case to the Christian community. One wonders how an individual could call oneself a Christian when demonstrating such split behavior, especially one who has been in the faith for an extended time or as a leader. The Jekylls and Hydes I have met over the years have come in all ages and sizes, but they have had one common denominator: They have been manipulators. They knew how to work the control dynamic to get what they wanted. They used words of guilt, shame, anger, put-downs, criticism, etc., on others to get what they wanted. Quite disturbing is that they used the hierarchy of the Christian faith to subjugate their wives.

The Christian faith indeed portrays the husband as the head of a marriage, but the understanding of headship is skewed by Mr. Hyde. Christian headship is about servanthood, which informs us that a Christian head is the one who should first show the way for what is required. The husband is to show his wife and family what humility looks like and how a submissive spirit is displayed. Such a Christian leader earns the personal respect of his wife and children; he doesn't demand it.

In George Orwell's book *1984*, Orwell suggests that language makes humans easy to control. Control the language, and you control the people.[27] The author of *Rules for Radicals* and political agitator Saul Alinsky writes, "Ridicule is man's most potent weapon ... for it infuriates the opposition."[28] A husband or wife with Hyde-like qualities will use pejorative language to control and manipulate.

Physical abuse may occur, but the emotional, psychological, and spiritual abuse is like the proverbial frog in the pot of tepid water. Sitting in a pot, before the water boils, all is well, and the

---

[27] George Orwell, *Nineteen Eighty-Four* (London: Secker and Warburg, 1949).

[28] Saul Alinsky, *Rules for Radicals* (New York: Random House, 1971), 128.

frog is clueless. The frog remains clueless as the heat slowly rises, and then it is too late for the frog to escape. Family and friends witnessing the effects of abuse on their loved one by Mr. or Mrs. Hyde raise the alarm to their loved one. But the abused spouse does not realize or recognize just how greatly the abuse has affected him or her until the abused spouse eventually wakes up and realizes that he or she is but a shell of their former self.

During Patty Hearst's kidnapping in 1974, she was held captive for nineteen months by a group of radical terrorists.[29] Ms. Hearst, a wealthy newspaper baron's granddaughter, was seen as a high-profile target by kidnappers. She became a sympathizer with her kidnappers' cause after being in their presence for an extended time, subjected to endless indoctrination in their point of view, and bombarded with criticism and disdain for her lifestyle of privilege. Sadly, in the same way, the spouse of a Mr. or Mrs. Hyde can be broken down over time to believe and accept the view of his or her abuser. What is the abuser's view? The spouse is gaslighted into believing that he or she is the source of all marital trouble. The "guilty" spouse is constantly accused of bringing trouble on himself or herself, and on to the very respectable Mr. or Mrs. Jekyll.

Is There Hope for Mr. or Mrs. Hyde?

Here is the million-dollar question: Can Mr. or Mrs. Hyde ever be reached and reformed? Yes, it is possible because, "With God, all things are possible" (Matthew 19:26). But is it probable? According to my findings, I lean toward the answer being no. Why? Because I do not think ignorance is what makes Mr. and Mrs. Hyde the person they are. They have free will, and they use it to control others. I believe the core issues inside the Hydes of

---

[29] "Patty Hearst," *Famous Cases & Criminals*, FBI, https://www.fbi.gov/history/famous-cases/patty-hearst.

life are pride and narcissism, which are extremely hard to counter. No one can convince the Hydes of the world that they are wrong. Fallout from that pride and narcissism keeps the Hydes on the move, along with the Dr. Jekylls. For Dr. Jekyll to retain the image of Dr. Jekyll, Mr. Hyde must remain hidden. When Mr. or Mrs. Hyde is revealed, in their thinking, it is time to move on. They become church hoppers. Such people believe they are being mischaracterized and maligned. I would see great hope in redeeming the Hydes of the world if they were forced to remain in one place after being exposed and humbled to the point of repentance. But within such a transient society, it is easy for people to move and relocate, which allows the Mr. and Mrs. Hydes to do so and continue to flourish as they are. Real change could happen if circumstances forced them to stay where they were accountable - exposed and in need to face themselves.

I once heard an applicable story about two brothers in England who were guilty of stealing sheep from a local pasture. As part of their punishment, each was prominently branded on the forehead with two large letters: ST, for sheep thief. The younger brother was so humiliated and ashamed that he moved away from the small town of his youth, to an area that did not know of his past. The older brother decided to stay in the town and live down the shame of his deed. Throughout the older brother's life, various people moved into the town, and new generations rose up. After the remaining brother left a store one day, a customer, new to the town, asked the store clerk, "I'm curious. Do you have any idea what those two letters ST mean on that gentleman's forehead who just left?

The clerk answered, "They are the abbreviation for the word *saint*, for there's no finer or more honest man in all of the county than him!" That's not Mr. Hyde. He doesn't like to stay around once exposed, and he doesn't see the need to change. To Mr. or Mrs. Hyde, it's always others who need to change.

What could possibly change Mr. or Mrs. Hyde, other than staying put and facing the music about his or her dual persona? I would guess that it would take a compilation of catastrophic events, such as a spouse leaving, ending in divorce(s), a loss of job or career, a serious health setback, growing old, loneliness, or anything that would strike hard against his or her pride and self-sufficiency. Even then, I have found some who would not change, regardless of the destruction they actually foisted upon themselves. They are satisfied in their thinking that they are never the cause, only the victim.

I have found a spouse's best hope of changing a controlling and gaslighting Mr. or Mrs. Hyde is to stand up to this persona, draw a line in the sand, and follow through with the stand you choose to take. I realize this is far easier said than done, but these three actions are the most effective means of turning around this marriage problem or rescuing a spouse from the enclosed walls that will stifle his or her self-worth.

Does it come with risks? Yes, it does. The Hydes may become more volatile. The Hydes may call their spouses' bluffs to see if they mean what they say. They may do so with a couldn't-care-less attitude, which allows and even dares their spouses to leave. But they will not let you go quietly or sometimes, at all. There may be children involved. If so, spouses must consider the cost of leaving compared with staying and risking the lasting effects of the Hyde persona on them.

Effects will happen whether you stay or go. What is best and right for you and your children should be paramount in your thinking and not what is inconvenient or hard. Help is out there for you. It will come as you need it. What could be worse than your children coming from a broken home? It is children growing up in a home where there *should* have been marital separation, otherwise irreparable harm could be visited upon the children exposed to a seriously dysfunctional home. Ongoing exposure to such a homelife will often leave children more damaged than living in a single-parent environment.

If you are married to this dual person, realize that the nature of hard has two sides. You already know that it is hard to live with such a volatile spouse. You also know that it would be hard to leave due to all the unforeseen uncertainties you would have to navigate. Which option offers you the best opportunity for a happily ever after life? With Mr. or Mrs. Hyde, you know what your future will be. If you decide to come out from under such marital abuse, it will be hard—at least at the beginning, but I suggest that if you do so you have a far better shot at recovery for yourself, your children, and the future. Do not allow yourself to remain trapped in a one-way marriage, where you are dedicated to displaying God-honoring conduct as a marriage partner while your mate exercises a Jekyll and Hyde persona. That does not constitute a good-faith marriage.

A major part of seeing yourself in the mirror of marriage is focusing on getting yourself right as a marriage partner and doing right by your mate. If your mate chooses not to do the same, he or she is in violation of not following through with the spirit required of a good-faith marriage. This is promoted and promised in the wedding ceremony. I believe the Bible presents and teaches a good-faith marriage. When a partner fails to practice such, that partner violates God's standard for married individuals. I appeal to 2 Peter 1:20-21, where we are informed that no scripture is to be interpreted by isolating any text. We need proper exegesis, where all Scripture is studied for a proper understanding of any text. When the scriptures are taken as a whole, I believe we can conclude that God does not require a spouse to sit under abuse by his or her mate.

Hopefully, what you see in the marriage mirror from this chapter is an image of a strong person, one who will stand up for oneself and not allow a spouse to take advantage of you. If the mirror reflects back to you a broken person, I would strongly suggest you consider making the changes to reclaim yourself from the domination of another.

CHAPTER 15

The Need for Renewal

A KEY THEME THREADED THROUGHOUT the Bible addresses the issue of renewal, and our need for it in order to keep on keeping on in life, regardless of what life throws at us. After facing yourself in the mirror of marriage and seeing what you saw, more than likely you uncovered some areas in your life and marriage that need adjusting. Hopefully you haven't discovered the need for a complete overhaul of oneself, but whatever conclusions you came to, the hope is that there will be a positive outcome to what you had revealed about yourself.

Our defeats and failures too often leave us hurting, helpless, and hopeless - at the bottom of an endless pit— especially when those failures are of a relational or marital nature, Much of life calls for renewal in some form. The Bible speaks of *re*joicing, which is another way of saying that our joy needs to be *re*visited, and brought back into our lives. The same is true when the Bible tells us to *re*member, or bring things back into our thinking that we have forgotten.

To be *re*newed means to be made new again, or *re*stored, and that's what can happen for you as a wife or husband that wants to get back the relationship you may have lost over the course of your marriage, or are now in danger of losing. Return to the days of your marriage, when before all the baggage that divided you got in the way of the relationship. Correct your wrongs and start again in the spirit of being renewed in your heart and resolve. Putting forth your best effort can give you hope of rescuing and restoring your marriage, if it's in danger of collapse.

And if your marriage is not in danger of collapse, renewing and restoring yourself to the person your spouse originally fell in love with will be the best guardian against your marriage heading in the wrong direction. God's Word is our light, and the mirror is our willingness to be seen as we are and to expose areas in our lives yet needing work. I close with a personal adaptation of part of the "Serenity Prayer."[30]

> God, thank You for the power to change things
> that I can;
> To work on the things only I can change;
> And wisdom to know what to do with the difference.

And what if your marriage can't be salvaged, due to an unwillingness on your spouse's part to be accepting of your newfound efforts? Or perhaps your spouse has no interest in changing those things about him or herself that is the major source of marital conflict and damage? Then renewal will have a different face for you. You will need to either go on in your marriage as a "new" person in hopes that down the road your personal changes within yourself will pay dividends in turning your spouse around, or you will choose to move on in life, past a marriage that could not be salvaged. Renewal can also involve new beginnings, and that may be the road you choose or need to take. But in doing so, you move forward as a changed and better person that what you were.

---

[30] Reinhold Niebuhr, "Prayer for Serenity," *Celebrate Recovery: A Christ-Centered 12-Step Program*, https://www.celebraterecovery.com/resources/cr-tools/serenityprayer.

Conclusion

Looking in the mirror is a daily routine for many who need to rise, shine, and get ready for work. They want to look their best as they leave home, and using a mirror is one way of checking for that. In this book, you have been using the mirror of marriage to see your true self on the inside, which eventually projects through you to your outside. The purpose of this book is to help you do that by revealing the lives of my wife and me in our marriage walk and by penning insights and lessons learned while engaged in the counseling trenches for over five decades. Two beggars (Joni and I), in the early years of our marriage, were provided bread (insights) by others along our journey. Now we are showing another beggar (you) where to find bread. I hope you have found and partake of the bread necessary to feed and nourish a successful marriage. God bless you.

APPENDIX 1

The Twenty-Five As of an Awesome Marriage

Above all, keep fervent in your love for one another, because love covers a multitude of sins. (1 Peter 4:8)

Fervent: "to stretch"[31]

Directions

1. Each spouse takes a sheet of paper and makes two columns, side-by-side, with each column going from the top of the page to the bottom of the page. Number from 1 to 25 down each column. Above the first column, put your name. Above the second column, put the name of your spouse.

2. On a scale of 0–5, enter in column one the appropriate number next to each *A* as you go down the list on your sheet of paper and evaluate yourself. The better you think

---

[31] William Vine, "Fervent, Fervently," *Vine's Expository Dictionary of New Testament Words,* Blue Letter Bible, https://www.blueletterbible.org/search/dictionary/viewtopic.cfm.

you do each *A*, the higher the number you put next to each *A*.

3. In column two, put the appropriate number next to each *A* that reflects how well you think your spouse does or doesn't do each particular *A*. The better the *A* is done, the higher the score (based on a 0-5 scale).

4. As a couple, add the total number from your two columns, and add the numbers from your spouse's two columns. Now add the four columns together, and then divide by two.

5. The final number after dividing by two reflects the status of your marriage, as seen and represented by both parties. Now compare your bottom-line number to the corresponding number found below, under **"Combined Score Total Meanings."**

6. After completing the exercise, discuss your findings with each other. Commit to working on the necessary adjustments to make your marriage what it ought to be— both honoring to God and a satisfying experience for both spouses.

Combined Score Total Meanings

250	Maximum score (No marriage will be perfect)
187 and above	Your marriage has earned standout status!
151–187	You are on the path to a very good marriage.
125–150	You have an average marriage.
62–125	There is a lot of missing work in your marriage.

This exercise will also show you how differently a couple in a marriage views the marriage. Most likely, when a husband adds up the two columns on his paper, you will find that he registers a higher score than the two columns the wife added up on her paper. Husbands are often surprised that the wives register a lower number when they assess, and the wives are surprised the husbands register a higher number in their views. Generally speaking, this is a case of husbands thinking their marriages are good and wives feeling their marriages leave a lot to be desired. All along, wives may have been telling their husbands of their wish for better, closer, and more fulfilling marriages, but wives have felt it didn't register in the minds of their husbands. During that time, husbands have been sailing along in marriage, thinking all is well on the home front.

For both spouses, wake up, smell the roses, and be open to what you hear through this exercise. If I were a betting man, which I am not, my money would be on both mates being surprised about the things they learn about themselves in this exercise, no matter how long they have been married.

The scoring system is based on conclusions that I came to when matching findings culled from my counseling experience and perspective over the years regarding how well the "Twenty-Five As" reflected the state of various marriages, including mine, that I have dealt with. This exercise and the material within it should be viewed as a viable tool that can be helpful in assessing one's marital success, but it is not based on any scientific case study. One should view this as a virtual assessment of one's marriage.

It would be wise to engage in this exercise from time to time, for I have found results may fluctuate depending on one's feelings during a moment, which can be influenced due to growth or regression in the marriage relationship. Stay on top of your marriage. Don't let it develop a leak like a slowly deflating tire.

The Test

(Twenty-Five *A*s of an Awesome Marriage)

1. Attentive

+ From time to time, I employ different surprises for my spouse, such as giving special cards or flowers, taking my spouse out to eat, implementing a night out at the movies, going on a weekend getaway or day trips, cooking my spouse's favorite meal, or making his or her favorite dessert.

2. Affectionate

+ I kiss my spouse when separating for work, and I kiss my spouse when coming back together. I promote thoughtful gestures, such as holding hands or rubbing my partner's back, shoulders, or feet, or initiate romantic moments.

3. Alternating

+ I make sure we take turns in activities so that my choices won't dominate the marriage.

4. Affirming

+ I speak (not just think) words of appreciation about and to my mate. I work at recognizing the good in my partner and the good my partner does for me and others.

5. Approving

+ My overall demeanor shows that I like what I have. I am proud to be with my mate, and I show it in various ways.

6. Admiring

+ I attempt to do the things that earn my mate's admiration. I work hard, help others, and am a giver. I believe my Christian walk is respected by my mate.

7. Attractive (Nonphysical)

+ I keep a positive attitude and a sense of humor. I work at having a pleasing personality.

8. Attractive (Physical)

+ I keep myself desirable regarding hygiene, grooming, weight, and dress. I understand that aging and circumstances can bring weight and health challenges, but I try my best to look my best.

9. Actions

+ I make positive deposits into our love account by doing things I know will please and are important to my mate.

10. Accepting

+ I accept the foibles in my mate because I see him or her exerting effort to overcome those foibles.

11. Adjusting

+ I give reasonable latitude to my mate's idiosyncrasies. I don't allow those traits to push my buttons.

12. Attitude

+ I stay positive. I don't allow the disappointments of life and the hard work that a successful marriage requires to swallow my attitude.

13. Audio

+ I talk and listen. I don't clam up, and I don't interrupt.

14. Apology/Acknowledgment

+ I confess my faults when I am wrong. I own my wrongs, and I do it without the qualifier, "But ..."

15. Adventuresome

+ I don't lose the excitement for life. I'm not a couch potato. I make an effort to try new things, as my spouse would suggest.

16. Aligning

+ I align my attitude and perspective with the good things of my marriage. I don't let problems and disagreements take center stage and overshadow the many good things that have and are happening in our marriage.

17. Analyzing

+ I am working on earning a PhD in my mate. I am endeavoring to learn everything I can through observation, listening, asking, and sensing.

18. Accommodating

+ I give my mate latitude to enjoy life as my mate wishes. I support my mate's positive pursuits. I don't bad-mouth or dismiss what my mate enjoys.

19. Acquiescing

+ I do my fair share of giving in and letting go. I don't always have to win and have things my way. I compromise.

20. Allocating

+ I stay in my lane. As a wife, I don't mother my husband by telling him what to do, how to do it, when to do it, or why to do it. As a husband, I don't treat my wife as a subordinate or make her feel incompetent. I am careful to allow my mate to operate in his or her own way and timing.

21. Anticipating

+ I do a good job of recognizing the approaching signs of a bad day for my mate. I give space and grace.

22. Altruistic

+ I demonstrate selfless behavior by sacrificing my interests for the benefit and well-being of my mate so that he or she can have or do what he or she wants.

23. Approachable

+ My mate can approach me about anything. I don't give off vibes that intimidate my mate.

24. Allegiance

+ I show my mate that nothing in my life (outside of Christ) is more important than my mate—not sports, children, money, friends, fitness, my mother, or my father.

25. Assessment/Appraisal

+ Every so often, I promote a checkup on the status of our marriage. I'll ask if anything I'm doing frustrates my mate or if I need to work on something.

The Twenty-Five Bs of a Broken Marriage

All of us, from time to time, slip up in our relationships due to our humanness. What I am addressing here is chronic wrong behavior. This damaging conduct shows often enough that it raises the red flag of concern in the mind.

Directions

1. In this exercise, circle the *B*s present in your marriage. Circle the *B*s you are responsible for and put a check mark next to each *B* for which you believe your spouse is responsible.
2. Displaying any of these *B*s can jeopardize the health and longevity of your marriage. Having a handful of them—even a small handful—in your relationship should raise the alarm that it could threaten any chance for a happy marriage.
3. If you choose to have your spouse participate in this exercise, do so with caution, for your spouse may not appreciate the check marks you placed while rendering your assessment of him or her.

4. In light of this exercise, evaluate changes you need to make concerning your conduct. If your spouse participates, discuss your combined findings and make the necessary changes within yourselves,

In this test, there is no detailed scoring system. There is only a simple evaluation that reflects responses. The number of *B*s circled should give you ample understanding that clearly shows you the state of your marriage and the required work to make it a viable marriage.

Identify each "B" that raises a red flag of concern in your mind that you do or your spouse does.

Test

1. Blaming

+ I engage in the blame game: accusing, finger-pointing, and calling out my mate's mistakes, faults, and shortcomings.

2. Brooding

+ I am a moody person who withdraws often.

3. Brewing and Stewing

+ I allow unresolved conflicts to fester within myself.

+ I have lingering agitation over discussions or disagreements, but I keep it within.

4. Blowing/Blasting

+ I allow pent-up issues and feelings to develop to where I eventually explode.

5. Badgering/Belaboring

+ I nag and give constant reminders (I beat dead horses).

6. Baiting

+ At times, I itch for a fight and look for a trigger point. I try to push my mate's buttons.

7. Bruising

+ I physically abuse my mate by pushing or hitting him or her.

8. Battling

+ I engage in incessant arguments. I don't give up. I argue to win.

9. Body

+ I don't do well managing my personal hygiene and weight, and I know it bothers my spouse.

10. Belittling

+ I put down, mock, and deprecate my mate. I say things to hurt my spouse.

11. Busted Budgets

+ I live financially beyond our means and constantly keep us in debt.

12. Baggage

+ I won't let go of hurt and past issues done to me by my spouse.

+ I won't let go of things from my spouse's past that happened before we met.

13. Bottle

+ I drink a lot of alcohol

14. Beauties/Beaus

+ I maintain relationships with the opposite sex, that my spouse disapproves of.

15. Bullying/Belligerent

+ As a husband, I play the headship card a lot.

+ As a wife, I push an independent, or resistant, spirit.

16. Bellicose

+ I show a hostile spirit of aggressive behavior and a willingness to fight.

17. Buffaloed

+ I blow a lot of hot air by engaging in empty arguments—against facts, evidence, or logic—to confuse or convince my spouse to get my way, or to cover a wrong.

18. Bothered

+ I show by my actions or attitudes that I don't like my mate. I get annoyed at my mate's antics, habits, questions, or personality.

19. Bitter

+ I allow being bothered to turn into becoming bitter.

20. Besieged

+ My spouse constantly feels inundated, overwhelmed, and weighed down by my attitude or actions.

21. Befuddle

+ I purposely muddy the waters in discussions by adding superfluous material, which brings confusion to the discussion.

22. Bemoan

+ I am constantly showing and/or speaking discontent.

23. Bereft

+ I don't give praise or appreciation to my spouse.

24. Busy

+ I get involved in too many things, while my spouse, family, and home duties are left wanting.

25. Betwixt

+ I get caught between options, and I don't make decisions in a timely manner, which frustrates my spouse.

The Twenty-Five Cs for Connecting in Communication

Communication is never the problem in marriage because communication happens 24-7 in life and marriage. The more critical issue is being able to identify *what* a person *is* communicating. Refusing to talk is communication. Withdrawal is communication. Glares and stares are communication. Looks of disdain are communication. Road rage is communication. Smiles are communication, as are hugs and handshakes.

We usually communicate something, but we do not necessarily connect. Sometimes people can misread us, and at times, we misread others. There is a difference between communication, which happens virtually all the time, and *connection,* which happens only when all parties interact to the point of connecting the dots. Some might suggest that the difference between communicating and connecting is splitting hairs and that they are virtually one and the same. I believe there is a nuanced distinction, and it is enough to make a difference.

Communication

The exchange of information or opinions. [32]

Communication is done verbally and nonverbally. It is done by watching, reading, and listening to people, feeling vibes, and assessing things. You use not only the ears or eyes but also the other senses. What you observe in others communicates something to you about them. How you feel around someone communicates something to you and perhaps also about that other person.

Spouses talk back and forth with each other, but quite often, it ends up being talking *at* each other, as in an argument. And even more, couples talk *past* each other. In these situations, communication *has* taken place. The communication that happens might be misunderstanding, frustration, venting, anger, or confusion, but there has been communication. What is missing is connection.

Connection

Bond, link. [33]

Connection Killers

On a scale of 0-5 (5 being a lot), put the number next to each of the listed killers as it reflect you. After the slash mark, (/), put the number that you think best represents your spouse. Example: 3/1.

_____ Controlling: micromanaging the relationship
_____ Condescending: conveying a sense of superiority
_____ Crabby or Cranky: irritable or ill-tempered

---

[32] · "Communication," *Merriam-Webster.com Dictionary*, https://www. merriam-webster.com/dictionary/communication.

[33] · "Connection," *Merriam-Webster.com Dictionary*, https://www.merriam-webster.com/dictionary/connection.

_____ Convoluted: talking all over the place, in a hard-to-follow way, or off subject

_____ Calculating: acting in a scheming way

_____ Complacent: showing smug satisfaction with oneself and one's achievements

_____ Complaining: expressing dissatisfaction or annoyance

_____ Comparison: the negative kind

_____ Capricious: sudden and/or unaccountable changes in mood or behavior

_____ Cold: lacking emotion or warmth

_____ Callous: insensitive or cruel

_____ Condemning: strong expression of disapproval; to censure

_____ Careless (care less): with one's words, attitudes, or actions

_____ Competitive: in a destructive way

_____ Contempt: a disregard for what should be considered

A high score obviously is not healthy. Go to work on lowering your score to better connect with each other in the marriage.

Healthy Vitamin C Promoters

The more good Cs you have, the more you'll connect in communication. On a scale of 1–5 (5 being excellent), put the number to the left of each heading word that accurately reflects how well you practice each C. Using the same scale, have your mate (if both are willing) also put a number to the right of each C, which he or she believes best reflects you.

If the spouse is willing, follow the above guidelines and do the same exercise for him or her that was done on you.

Caring

+ I am intentional in taking time to talk, interact, and show that I care.

+ I take time to listen to something that may not be of interest or an issue to me.

Careful

+ I guard against rolling my eyes, giving a half-smile, projecting negative facial expressions, disrespectfully turning away, chronically being in a hurry, and having a combative spirit.

+ I don't miss the underlying tone that my spouse may give off.

+ I am careful to hear beyond words. I listen for intent, spirit, hurt, need to vent, and excitement.

+ I am not an intransigent person whose focus is only, "But that's what you said!"

+ I don't overly focus on my mate's words and miss my mate's heart and intent (Some people are not good with words or at expressing thoughts).

Concentrating

+ I am careful to maintain eye contact when talking and listening.

+ I don't look around in a way that gives the impression of disinterest or having divided attention.

Considerate

+ I don't interrupt my mate mid-sentence.

+ I don't give the impression that I'm not listening (possibly guilty because my focus is on making my next point).

+ I don't project the impression that I can't wait to talk.

+ I show respect by being "slow to speak and quick to hear" (James 1:19).

+ I don't condescend or patronize when I talk to my mate.

+ I thoughtfully consider where my mate is at the moment; they may be coming off a hard day.

+ I am alert to where a discussion is headed, and I proceed with caution.

+ I actively remember that we are different.

Compare

+ I don't negatively compare my spouse to others.

Compassion

+ I give my mate latitude to vent as needed.

+ I remember the beatitude of mercy (See Matthew 5:7).

+ I don't come across as cold, hard, or an emotionless stone.

Continuous

+ I continually talk (the good kind and not the nagging or annoying kind).

+I continue to try to engage, even though my spouse stops talking and appears to show no interest in listening.

Clarity/Clarify/Concise

+ I work at being clear in understanding what my mate wants or wants to say.

+ I don't make my mate play the guessing game about what I'm after or what I really want.

+ Hidden messages don't underlie my words.

+ I don't mumble under my breath while walking away.

+ I double-check that I hear correctly on important matters.

+ I work at not being overly wordy.

Conversing

+ I practice taking turns in talking (no lectures).

+ I don't raise my decibel level when discussing. I remain conversational.

Confession/Contrition

+ When I have dropped the ball about something we discussed previously, I own it, and I don't excuse it or brush it off.

+ I apologize when my actions are wrong and affirm my partner for his or her right behavior.

Compromise

+ I make sure I do my fair share of compromising. I don't insist on things being my way.

Caution

+ I do not engage in hurtful name-calling.

+ I do not make sweeping generalities ("You always," or "You never").

+ I do not use pejorative language.

Contemplate

+ I take the time to prep myself by thinking through my words before difficult discussions.

+ Touchy subjects are thought through and are approached at an appropriate time and in a conducive setting.

+ I consider the mood/response/reaction in which a spouse will be left after a discussion.

Conscious

+ I am aware of how I come across.

+ I am aware there may be underlying issues that need to be identified.

Completion

+ I'm good at completing my thoughts.

+ I don't accumulate a list of incompletes while talking and not following through.

+ I guard against having many discussions with much talking but no resolutions.

+ I don't leave discussions dangling over long periods of time.

Closure

+ I put to bed things that have already been talked through instead of constantly revisiting and rehashing things that will cause irritation and separation.

Capitulating

+ I know when to quit and give it up, and I do it.

+ I am good at reading the tea leaves or the handwriting on the wall when it's time to back off.

+ I know when my spouse is becoming upset, and I try to assuage the situation.

Corralling

+ I'm careful not to allow myself to be a scatterbrain (all over the place in what I say).

+ I know that introducing too many subjects will muddy the water and cause a disconnect.

Camping

+ I don't beat a dead horse by staying on a discussion about an issue.

+ I don't lecture, nag, or regurgitate the same old issues, which lead to a shutdown by my mate.

Confirming

+ I put important decisions we discussed in writing (on a calendar or notepad).

Confronting

+ I confront my mate when I need to, without destroying the one I love.

+ I am careful when confronting areas of hard discussion (parenting, finances, roles in marriage, etc.)

Comforting

+ I use words that build up and don't tear down.

+ I use affectionate names for my mate like Honey, Sweetheart, My Love, and Puddle Cakes (just kidding on the last one).

+ I endeavor to reassure my spouse of my love.

Complimenting

+ I seek to build up my mate when he or she deserves well-earned praise.

+ The right behavior and effort of my spouse are noted and appreciated.

Constraint/Calm

+ I don't allow myself to get out of control.

+ I don't blame my mate for my lack of control.

Coherent/Cogent

+ I work at being logical and consistent in what I say and how I say it.

+ I don't lie, fudge, or use half-truths that don't add up or make sense.

+ I endeavor to make sense when articulating my points.

101-125 Outstanding connections in communication!

76-100 Excellent connections in communication

51-75 Good connections in communication

26-50 Hit & miss connections in communication

0-25 Your connections in communication are on life support

APPENDIX 4

99 Questions (and a few more) to ask Before an Engagement

As I mentioned earlier in the book, there is no Mr. or Mrs. Right out there that is the perfect mate for you. If we believe marriage doesn't create problems but rather reveals problems, it would be wise to know as much as you can ahead of time about your potential partner. It's important to recognize the problems in a potential mate before taking the big step of commitment. Then ask yourself this question: If the problems within my potential spouse-to-be remain unresolved, knowing what I know about myself, can I live with those problems?

Here is a list of ninety-nine issues you can go through to help you consider what you can and can't live with regarding a potential partner. Obviously, you can't absolutely know beforehand if you can live with what a partner brings to the marriage, but this list will help in knowing what you are getting into before you say, "I do."

You start out with one another as friends. As the friendship blossoms and progresses, you'll need to address some issues and answers *before* you ever consider engagement or being in a committed relationship.

How Does Each Person Answer or Feel about These Issues?

1. Have either of you been married before? If so, how many times?
2. What was the cause of any breakups in past relationships?
3. As a couple, have you broken up before? How many times? What was the cause?
4. Will the bride take the last name of her husband? If so, is this a point of contention?
5. Do both of you want children? If so, number of children each person hopes to have as a family? When does each desire the arrival of the first child?
6. Are both of you open to adoption?
7. If given a choice, where is the ideal place that each of you would want to live?
8. Will the mother return to the outside work world after giving birth? Do both of you agree that the mother is to return to the outside work world, and how soon?
9. What are the methods of discipline each of you will use with the children? Is spanking acceptable to each parent?
10. In what faith will the children be reared?
11. Is each of you currently a consistent church attendee? Do each of you plan to be a consistent church attender? Which denomination will you attend?
12. What is each of you: early-to-bed-and-early-to-rise people, or night owls?
13. Will either of you bring any debt to a marriage?
14. Is there any ongoing debt obligation being brought to the marriage (child support, school debt, etc.)?
15. Have you both seen a good marriage model in your respective parents?
16. Are there any children from a prior relationship?
17. Does either of you have shared custody with an ex-spouse? What's the arrangement?

18. Are both of you committed to sexual purity until marriage (not being roommates regardless of how convenient or how much money you can save in preparation for marriage)?
19. Are either of you considered a tightwad or a spendthrift?
20. Has either of you been a victim of sexual abuse?
21. Has either of you been a perpetrator of sexual abuse?
22. Do parents and friends approve of your relationship? If not, why not?
23. Do either of you have a habit of living beyond your financial means?
24. Do either of you have financial savings and a savings plan? A pre-nup?
25. Will finances be jointly held or separated?
26. Who will be in control of the finances, and to what extent (writing checks, balancing the checkbook, etc.)?
27. Are either of you a neat-and-clean freak, somewhat of a slob, or neither?
28. Do either of you tend to hoard?
29. Do you have a Type A personality or a laid-back personality?
30. Is either of you a private person or a people person?
31. Do you both value exercise? To what point are you committed to it?
32. Do you pray together?
33. Does either of you have a temper problem? To what extent do you have it?
34. What is the biggest fear each of you has about marriage (other than a fear of it not working out)?
35. Does either of you speak insulting words to the other (never, sometimes, or often)?
36. What does each enjoy more: the journey or arriving at the destination?
37. What is the hardest part of your relationship? How is it shown?

38. Does each of you know the other person's favorite color?
39. Are either of you an avid sports fan?
40. What is the happiest part of your relationship, besides being together?
41. Does either of you watch television and movies? To what extent?
42. What do you consider is the best marriage advice you have heard?
43. Are either of you tethered to the electronic world? To what extent?
44. Does each of you like to mostly eat at home or out?
45. Are either of you a health-food nut or a junk-food addict?
46. Are you a vegan or a meat eater?
47. What is the biggest cause of your arguments?
48. What animal best reflects who you are?
49. What animal would your potential mate say best reflects you?
50. What animal would you say best describes your potential mate?
51. What animal would your potential mate say best describes him or her?
52. What is the biggest thing each of you would like to see the other change?
53. What is the biggest change you believe you need to make within yourself?
54. Who will have the last word in home decorating?
55. Based on your history, how *will* (not *should*) each of you handle strong disagreements with each other (stand your ground, acquiesce, compromise, or another way)?
56. Can your potential mate have close female and male friends?
57. Does either of you consume alcohol? If so, is it on occasion, daily, moderately, or heavily?

58. Have both of you been morally faithful? If not, has it been discussed and resolved?
59. Has either of you been emotionally abusive to the other? If so, how frequently?
60. Has either ever been physically abusive to the other? If so, how frequently?
61. Do you trust each other, or have trust issues surfaced?
62. How important to each of you are possessions (little, moderate, or very important)?
63. How does each of you handle emotional hurt (withdraw, clam up, argue, or yell)?
64. How good is each of you at owning your wrong (you acknowledge it, drag your feet, deflect it, defend it, or ignore it)?
65. Will there be pets in the home?
66. How difficult is it for each of you to forgive?
67. What is your greatest character flaw?
68. What do you consider to be your potential mate's greatest character flaw?
69. Has either of you, now or ever, been into pornography (from dabbling to addiction)?
70. What is the best thing you like about each other?
71. What is the relationship like between your potential mate and his or her parents?
72. What is the relationship like between you and your potential mate's parents?
73. Are you both OK with giving or lending money to family members or friends? To what extent?
74. How have things changed in your relationship, from your first days together to the present day?
75. How does each of you respond to stress?
76. Does each of you show respect to the other? If so, how do you show it?

77. Does either of you get annoyed with the other (never, seldom, many times, or all the time)?
78. Does either of you try to isolate the other from family and friends?
79. Does either of you criticize the other (never, seldom, often, or always)?
80. What net income do you think you need to have the lifestyle you want?
81. Where will you both spend the major holidays each year?
82. How will each of you resolve impasses of major importance (spending, debt obligation, disciplining children, where to live, etc.)?
83. What will you do if your potential husband doesn't show up as a biblically based spiritual leader, even after your reminders?
84. What will you do if your potential mate refuses to demonstrate a biblically based, submissive spirit?
85. What will you do if your potential wife or husband shows a controlling spirit, but he or she will not go to counseling?
86. Who compromises most in the relationship? To what percent is this true?
87. Does either of you bring up the past in a negative way?
88. Does either of you battle depression? If so, is it rarely, sometimes, often, or quite often? Do you take medication for it?
89. Do you both work hard at keeping an attractive physical appearance for each other?
90. Do you think your potential mate is a time waster (somewhat or quite a bit)?
91. Does your potential mate see you as a time waster (somewhat or quite a bit)?
92. Does either of you put the other person down (uses derogatory names, belittles, curses, etc.)?

93. Does either of you use body language conveying contempt toward the other (rolling the eyes, smirking, lifting arms in disgust, etc.)?
94. Does either of you have a problem with follow-through (sometimes, half the time, or usually)?
95. Does either of you have a tone in your voice that irritates the other? If so, how would you describe it?
96. Can each marry the other person just the way he or she is, assuming there may never be any change?
97. How does either of you feel about animals being a part of the home? What are acceptable animals, and how many do you want?
98. Are there political differences that could create trouble in the marriage? If so, how involved does each of you want to be politically?
99. According to you, outside of infidelity, what action(s) or inaction(s) would most threaten to destroy your marriage?

Printed in the United States
by Baker & Taylor Publisher Services